DEDICATION:

This Book is dedicated to mother,
who taught me to read, and insisted I should
always be well informed.

ACKNOWLEDGEMENTS:

Special Thanks to:
Sheldan Nidle and Patrick H. Bellringer

Their materials have been quoted most often,
and are important to this book.

SPECIAL THANKS TO:

Judi D. Johnson
For Art Work & Cover Design

Order this book online at www.trafford.com
or email orders@trafford.com

Most Trafford titles are also available at major online book retailers.

Print information available on the last page.

ISBN: 978-1-4251-7202-2 (sc)

Trafford rev. 05/01/2019

 www.trafford.com

North America & international
toll-free: 1 888 232 4444 (USA & Canada)
fax: 812 355 4082

TABLE OF CONTENTS

Chapter #   **Page #**

     Introduction & Background - - - - - - - - - - - - - -   1

1   Suppressed Science, Technology & Inventions -   4

2   Suppressed Medicines (Pharmaceutical Co.'s) - 29

3   Extraterrestrials, MJ12, Assassination, etc. - - - 49

4   Media, Secrecy, Lies & Suppression - - - - - - - - 65

5   Dumbing Down The Human Race - - - - - - - - - 75

6   Other Civilizations In Our Region
        of The Galaxy - - - - - - - - - - - - - - - - - 88

7   Ancient History of Planet Earth,
        prior to the flood - - - - - - - - - - - - - - - - 131

8   More Recent History, since the flood - - - - - - - - 141

9   Anti-Gravity Craft, built for U.S.
        Secret Government - - - - - - - - - - - - - - 146

10   Questions & Concerns - - - - - - - - - - - - - - - - - 152

11   What's Coming Down The Pike ? - - - - - - - - - - 155

12   How Big Is The Mushroom Problem ? - - - - - - - 159

13   illuminati To Be Killed For Creating
        Diseases To Kill Asians - - - - - - - - - - - 181

14   Star Nations Warn illuminati Concerning
Nuclear Devices & Pollution by Hydro-
Carbon Fuels etc. - 184

15   What About Our Legal Systems ? - - - - - - - - - - 189

16   A Real New Year's Day & Gov't Fears ET's - - - 192

17   Humanoid Immigrants to Earth ? - - - - - - - - - - 196

18   Unified Field Theory Suppressed - - - - - - - - - - 198

19   Time Machines, U/G Bases, & Human Clones- - 207

20   Dark Side Losing, Changes Coming,
                & NESARA - - - - - - - - - - - - - - 214

21   Canada's Income Tax
              Legislation, Practice, & Legality? - - - - - 222

22   Suggested Sources of Unbiased
              &Truthful Information - - - - - - - - - - - - - 229

FORWARD

THE MUSHROOM PROBLEM

The "Media" has been telling you that there is no "conspiracy". If you believe that, you have been led down the garden path. It is only a matter of a short time until you come to a shocking conclusion. You have been lied to, and set up as a dumb bunny or a sucker (or a mushroom) as soon as your "birth certificate" was issued. The web of deceit is broader & far more complex than you can imagine.

You are being dealt with, as a corporate entity by a government which is a corporation, where your courts are Admiralty Courts, and your statute law is adjudicated on the basis of the Uniform Commercial Code. You are a chattel or a commodity item of the state. This relates back to earlier laws regarding slaves..

Your highest level leaders, like Prime Minister or President, and quite often, the more important cabinet ministers, directors and secretaries of your government are paid off, owned and/or controlled by a higher and hidden level of Satanic / Luciferian controllers. That is not new at all. It has been going on since Christ was crucified. This hidden secret control and direction has been continuously carried out by the successors of the Pharisees, Royalty, Banking & Secret Societies for 2000+ yrs.

The illuminati, a secret society with members of the above groups, presently control all governments in developed countries, along with virtually all of their media. This has been done through the upper levels of related secret societies and organizations as well as many of the descendants of the Khazarian Zionist Jews, who are not originally of Hebrew descent, and became the Pharasees a long time ago. It is bothersome to note that the Arabs are far more "Semitic" (direct descendants of the Hebrews) than they are.

It is hard to believe that such secret Luciferian and Satanic control begins with the Jesuits at the top. The sequence is the Jesuits, illuminati, Freemasons, Skull & Bones, Scroll & Key, and other university secret societies tied back to the Freemasons, then the Bilderbergers, Royal families of England and Europe, the Committee of 300, the Council on Foreign Relations, NSA, CIA, FBI, Trilateral Commission. The judges in our courts, and virtually all of our leaders in government are usually 32nd. level and up, in the Freemasons. Any person who cannot be quietly and directly controlled by the illuminati, could not become a judge or a government leader, the way things are structured & controlled.

As you proceed through this book there will be references to The Protocols of The Learned Elders of Zion, which have been revealed in books by Henry Ford and William Cooper, respectively. The illuminati follow those protocols. **The Jesuit "Black Pope" ordered the assassination of the first Roman Catholic president of the United States of America. Catholics in the U.S. should get to know this.**

Our lying media and bought politicians have been telling you that gun control is essential to reducing criminal activity of all kinds, they were leaving out their own, and could not be more completely lying when they say the crime rates will drop.

"Don't eat that one Elmer, it's not what you think it is."

The following short and very high impact article is being quoted directly from the popular free and honest information website, www.rense.com , which is tied back to Jeff Rense's radio talk show. The website gets 10 million hits per month.

A LITTLE GUN HISTORY LESSON

March 7th., 2008.

* In 1929, the Soviet Union established gun control. From 1929 to 1953, about 20 million dissidents, unable to defend themselves, were rounded up and exterminated. This doesn't include the 30 million "Uncle Joe" starved to death in the Ukraine.

* In 1911, Turkey established gun control. From 1915 to 1917, 1.5 million Armenians, unable to defend themselves, were rounded up and exterminated.

* Germany established gun control in 1938 and from 1939 to 1945, leaving a populace unable to defend itself against the Gestapo and SS. Hundreds of thousands died as a result.

* China established gun control in 1935. From 1948 to 1952, 20 million political dissidents, unable to defend themselves were rounded up and exterminated.

* Guatamala established gun control in 1964. From 1964 to 1981, 100,000 Mayan Indians, unable to defend themselves, were rounded up and exterminated.

* Uganda established gun control in 1970. From 1971 to 1979, 300,000 Christians, unable to defend themselves, were rounded up and exterminated. The total dead are said to be 2 - 3 million.

* Cambodia established gun control in 1956. From 1975 to 1977, 1 - 2 million "educated" people, unable to defend themselves, were rounded up and exterminated.

* Defenseless people rounded up and exterminated in the 20th Century because of gun control = 56 million, at a bare min.

* Gun owners in Australia were forced by new law to surrender 640,381 personal firearms to be destroyed by their own government, a program costing Australian taxpayers more than $500 million dollars. The first year results = > > >

* Australia-wide, homicides went up 3.2 percent.

* Australia-wide, assaults went up 8.6 percent.

* Australia-wide, armed robberies went up 44 percent.
(yes, 44 percent)

In the state of Victoria alone, homicides with firearms are now up 300 percent. Note that while the law-abiding citizens turned them in, the criminals did not, and criminals still possess their guns.

It will never happen here? I bet the Aussies said that too.

While figures over the previous 25 years showed a steady DECREASE in armed robbery with firearms, that changed drastically upward in the first year after gun confiscation.. Since criminals now are guaranteed that their prey is unarmed.

There has also been a dramatic increase in break-ins and assaults of the ELDERLY. Australian politicians are at a loss to explain how the public safety has decreased, after such monumental effort and expense was expended in successfully ridding Australian society of guns. The Australian experience and the other historical facts above prove it.

You won't see this data on the U.S. evening news, or hear politicians disseminating this information. (Most of us north of the border, in Canada, can attest to the same

kind of reactions by media and politicians here, and only a Canadian "mushroom" wouldn't have noticed that by now.) Canada's negative results are being hidden & lied about, as much as possible at the moment ...

Guns in the hands of honest citizens save lives and property and, yes, gun-control laws adversely affect only the law-abiding citizens.

Jeff Rense suggests: "Take note my fellow Americans, before it's too late."

The next time someone talks in favor of gun control, please remind him of this history lesson. **With guns, we are "Citizens". Without them, we are "Subjects".**

During World war II, the Japanese decided not to invade America because they knew most Americans were ARMED.

Note: Admiral Yamamoto who crafted the attack on Pearl Harbor had attended Harvard University 1919 -1921 & was Naval Attache' to the U.S. 1925 - 28. Most of our navy was destroyed at Pearl Harbor and our army had been deprived of funding and was ill prepared to defend the country.

It was reported that when asked why Japan did not follow up the Pearl Harbor attack with an invasion of the U.S. mainland, his reply was that he had lived in the U.S. and knew that almost all households had guns.

If you value your freedom, please spread this anti-gun control message to all of your friends.

http://us.rd.yahoo.com/evt=51438 - http://www.yahoo.com/r/hs

As we continue beyond the above quoted article, here are a few facts. You are probably unaware of certain things, as not shown or reported in any of your controlled media, or mentioned at all by your government or politicians.

These revelations may get you seriously started toward greater awareness. They might also serve as a warning of what is coming at you, if someone does not stop its relentless progress. I suspect that all of the following things have been, and continue to be set up toward our planned enslavement.

More than 600 concentration camps in the U.S. - Nobody can convince me that those were set up to accommodate "illegal aliens", although some of the bullshit may suggest such a use. (It would be the same lying B.S. as with "gun control".)

More than 131 underground bases in the U.S. for various "secret" purposes, including DUMB (deep underground military bases), prison and concentration camp facilities. All of that information has been quietly obtained and published by a couple of brave folks. One of them was assassinated before his third published account could be distributed. Your secret government now has the ability to carve out more than 10 miles per day of fresh ceramic lined tunnels. The last quiet figure I heard for underground facilities, was said to be 1,500, and that person had been inside and had worked in some of them.

The CIA has controlled the world drug trade for about the last 50 years, and the take from that source has paid for all of those underground facilities, plus all of the secret stuff at Area 51, and more than ½ dozen types of anti-gravity craft. When the government says that has to be kept secret, that is B.S.. Russia has had exceptionally well-developed anti-gravity craft, capable of lifting 50 tons each, since at least 1982. Who in the hell is hiding from whom?? No need to wonder why I am writing this book. It is really **MUSHROOM** medicine.

Author's Biographical Note:

Born in Canada. Both parents were second generation Canadians of Icelandic descent. Dad taught me honesty, and to do my best at anything I do, and not to be sloppy or messy. A second or third class job was considered worse than not doing it at all in the first place. Mother taught me that my limitations were all most likely to be self-imposed, and that I could do anything that I wanted to do, as long as I wasn't too lazy or impatient to achieve the objective or goal.

I have worked at more than a dozen so-called occupations, up to and including extractive metallurgy. My inventions include a broad range of things from hydraulics to electrical, and chemistry to physics. My creations also include a few musical compositions and pieces of poetry, and some art work.

(The key has always been that you don't have to understand whatever it is you would like to do or create to start with. All you have to do is get on with it, learn all about it, and then create or conquer the thing you have set out to achieve.) That has always worked for me. I am stubborn enough to get there.

I am a senior citizen with a grown-up family, who are all in good health, and each is doing quite well at what they have chosen as an occupation. In that area in particular, I am very pleased, and believe I am most fortunate. Life is not just a matter of doing your own thing or owning or building better toys.

INTRODUCTION & BACKGROUND

Prior to 1964, I was already into a wide range of interesting subjects, including strange things in the world, unidentified flying objects and numerous other fascinating things. Not being interested in fiction, and having a strong desire to learn as much as possible beyond ordinary academic and "politically correct" subjects, large numbers of books were read. My wife and I have a collection of more than 3,500 books, including a large number exposing the One World Order Cabal, (Illuminati) and their lies, lies & more lies.

I have invented a number of new things, including a free energy device (many others have also invented such things) and a gasoline vaporizer with 300%+ potential, I have become aware of suppression and assassination. Those items have been put away until our system changes to where we inventors no longer face extermination for threatening the establishment and their absolute control over energy in particular. In the meantime, those criminals need to be exposed.

Our educational systems in the western world have been deliberately set up to discourage creative thinking as much as possible. I have seen published evidence of that fact, including a resolution passed by our "secret government" leaders in the 1950's. Our media, from newspapers to book publishers to radio and TV networks are now integral elements of a rather complete system of mind control by means of subterfuge, propaganda and outright lies. A high percentage of our population complacently believes, or simply tolerates those lies.

Our governments have progressively become fascist dictatorships, with virtually identical statutory legal systems based on the Uniform Commercial Code. We are treated in our courts as "the enemy" under a system of admiralty law, where you are guilty until proven innocent, not the other way around. Your country has mostly become a police state, as you may be suspecting by now.

A socialist dictatorship is Communism. A capitalist dictatorship is Fascism.

Who is behind this mushroom business? - A short condensed description

The Illuminati, a very old secret society of Satanists, included which until recent times have been 13 banking families who have controlled the world's money supply. They also are behind, and at top levels of most other world controlling organizations. The illuminati was founded & set up as an exclusive, closed Satanic society by the Jesuits.

The Illuminati are secretly behind and above all of the orders of Freemasons, and when one gets to 33rd. level of the Freemasons, that person becomes a member of the Illuminati. They are historically related to the "Khazarian" Jews. They were and are not Semites. They became the Pharisees -"The Money-Changers".

The Khazarians were the original "Zionists". Their long term world dictatorship plan is said to be "the protocols of the Learned Elders of Zion". Current observations would indicate that those protocols have been followed & carried out. The word "Nazi" relates to "Ashkanazi", another name for Khazarians.

False information and subtle systems of control at the present time cover a large number of subjects, such as agriculture, astronomy, energy, including oil & gas etc., government, organic and inorganic chemistry, medicine, physics, space & space travel, and many other things. When someone says "I don't believe that", the person making that statement usually does not know anything of any consequence about the subject, and probably has their head in the sand. Winston Churchill once said "mankind fights hardest to protect their own ignorance". (Hidebound folks seem to resist change with a vengeance).

Most people want a well-ordered and comparatively simple life, and could be easily led without question, as long as no outward violence is involved. They would follow each other until they fall into the sea and drown, like a bunch of lemmings. This book could become a wakeup call for a lot of those folks.

At the present time, well into the computer age, increasing numbers of people are waking up, paying attention, and finding out what is really going on. We are communicating with each other about the deceptions now being recognized, and many of us are now ready to do something about it, if we can.

As a so-called "senior citizen", I am computer literate, and thusly open to vast amounts of information on the internet. A serious majority of seniors are tied into mundane time consuming pursuits while being fed the usual bullshit and kept in the dark. If you as a reader of this book are 55 years of age or older, and have not attempted to obtain a personal computer (PC), and learned how to use it, you are just watching the world go by. You are missing out on the most fascinating, informing and entertaining media system ever created. It will broaden your horizons, and turn you into a more interesting person. You will be considered well informed and close to the action, rather than ending up being referred to as unaware of what is going on, by your younger contemporaries.

Virtually all of the information herein has been provided to and for me by many other researchers and authors, who deserve accolades for digging into things and coming up with the real answers. By referencing their books and articles, I hope to have my readers expand their knowledge by obtaining and reading the referenced books to the direct benefit of those authors.

Chapter 1

SUPPRESSED SCIENCE, TECHNOLOGY & INVENTIONS

Walter Russel - U.S.A.

In the 1920's, Walter Russell, a seriously capable person in the U.S., came up with a new and far more complete periodic table, indicating the male / female and companion nature of all of the elements. It is a completely balanced system of things interrelating elements which are likely to compound more easily. It covers a serious number of elements beyond those shown on the periodic table of elements now commonly used in our schools and universities. (160/106)

This new periodic table was published along with much further information, describing, detailing and diagramming how everything from solar systems to molecules and atoms all follow a similar logical order. The related descriptive material, diagrams and detail explanations also cover the geometry, behavior, interaction and general relationships between electricity, magnetism and gravity. In those descriptive discussions, a bar magnet is referred to as a gravity bar, and each bar magnet has 4 poles and not just 2. Also the force of gravity always assumes the shape of a spiral. It is the primary energy form, as well.

One of the main reasons why Walter Russell's works were totally suppressed, is that the information therein represents the keys to the control and harnessing of gravity, as well as principles to use to create free energy electrical generators. Some of us have been able to get Walter Russell's books, but not without searching for them. They suddenly became rather hard to find in the 1930's and 40's.

Ref: The Phoenix Journals - Book # 137 - dictated by St. Germain, - http://www.fourwinds10.com

Dr. Vladimir Gavreau - France

Dr. Gavreau, working on a French military project, researching the effects of low frequency sound waves, proved that an entire military division could be devastated in as little as 20 seconds through the use of low frequency sound projecting devices, set to the correct frequency. The French had decided to do this research based on the fact that the Nazis in Germany, prior to, and during World War 2, had developed devastating sound projection devices which could virtually demolish military tanks, etc...

There are obviously other more practical uses for the technology developed and perfected by Mr. Gavreau. Such further and more practical uses have been conveniently avoided, however, as the principles discovered and perfected resulted in weaponry far more effective and devastating than nuclear bombs. Our world controllers did not want that information to get out.

In the process of doing essential research on the subject, Gavreau learned that at various frequency levels, different effects were experienced by the human body. The Nazis used infrasound to extremely excite great crowds of people when Hitler was speaking to large gatherings. Reactions at varying frequencies, included confusion and other negative effects. At a certain critical frequency, with continued application for a few more seconds, such exposure would kill any person within target range, which extended for a great distance.

As a point of interest in connection with this low frequency sound situation, our military now always gets their marching soldiers to go out of step whenever they cross a bridge. The power of low frequency sound vibrations is so devastating that with the right cadence, the resonant frequency of the sound impulses from the marching soldiers would weaken the bridge, which could potentially collapse later under heavy load. Tesla had proven that with one of his early experiments before 1910. Another interesting discovery by Gavreau in his research was that the amount of applied input energy or wattage was very low for the devastating effect that was experienced on the receiving end. (Over-Unity?) Many times!!

It was also found that with proper focusing, low frequency sound waves could burst holes in military tanks with a body of thick steel. Further to that, it was also determined that aircraft could be downed quite easily with properly focused low frequency sound. An effective barrier or totally absorbing media was impossible to find in Gavreau's time.

Ref: "Lost Science" by Gerry Vassilatos.

Nicola Tesla - U.S.A.

To many in the U.S.A. and other countries, Nicola Tesla became famous as a great inventor. Folks are most familiar with the fact that Tesla was the original inventor designer and developer of electrical generators and motors which generated, or were powered by alternating current. Alternating current turned out to be far more efficient, easier to send over high voltage power transmission lines, and more convenient for the household, and electrocution was unlikely.
There was a far greater potential for electrocution with DC power, such as had been set up by Edison in New York, by the time Tesla was bringing out his AC system of things. The original massive A/C electrical generators which were installed at Niagara Falls were built to Tesla's specifications. Tesla's first activities with AC systems were under way in the 1890's. Tesla was a very prolific inventor, and eventually, by 1940 or thereabouts, he had filed somewhere in the order of 800 + patent applications. Tesla's other inventions aside from AC electrical devices included a great diversity of things.
Tesla was the original inventor of the radio, and won an infringement case against Marconi. He was also the original inventor of remote control devices which were radio controlled. He had proven by about 1903 that he could transmit vast amounts of electrical power in leaps of at least

28 miles, without wires. He had developed and demonstrated both the generating and receiving systems, and perfected them to the point that their transmission losses were lower than through the use of wires. Needless to say, those holding the economic power, were already then majority owners of the first public electrical utilities, and surely did not want to see any system adopted that would transmit electrical power without the use of wires. How were they going to monitor, or charge for the electrical energy, if that sort of system was adopted?

Around that time, J. Pierpont Morgan, and interrelated financiers controlling the utilities, began to assure that Edison was given all the accolades and Tesla was relegated to a level of obscurity. Tesla began to suggest, as early as 1900 or before, that it was surely there for the tapping, and he would eventually be able to produce a system which would provide free electrical power to everybody. Tesla had maintained an elaborate laboratory where his research and development work was done. At one point, when Tesla had perfected and was constantly improving upon his power transmission system without wires, and was refusing to be intimidated by Mr. Morgan and his cronies, Tesla's laboratory was burned to the ground. The fire was deliberately set. Morgan and Rockefeller were of Khazarian descent, and known to cause damage to, or create extreme problems for competitors.

As time progressed, Tesla invented a series of experimental free energy devices which picked up energy from the atmosphere and the ground, and converted it to useful electrical current. It is further known that in 1929, Tesla had converted an automobile to be driven by an electric motor, and had further placed a solid state free energy electrical generator under the hood.

This car was demonstrated at the time, and outperformed all other cars in existence. An electric motor has far more torque than a diesel engine, and is ridiculously efficient by comparison. The impact of that situation must have been horrendous, as far as the energy monopolists were concerned. Something like the impact on the Toronto stock market, when the public became aware that Pogue's carburetor could get up to 216 miles per Imperial gallon of gas.

Those demonstrations, and any related publication, were totally suppressed from that time forward. John D. Rockefeller senior, who was a close associate of Mr. Morgan, was already dominating the petroleum industry by that point in time.

Tesla was also the inventor of what became the modern standard ship's compass, also of most of the basic items of testing, metering and recording equipment related to the use and measurement of electrical energy. Among his odd inventions were what became the standard lightening rod, a humidifier, a highly efficient disc pump that worked on the basis of surface tension, and a steam turbine version of that pump which was also extremely efficient.

During and following his experiments with wireless transmission of electrical energy, Tesla found out that such power could be pulsed and focused. That technology was stolen by the powers in control of what was then quietly established as the "secret government" of the U.S.A.

Potential for scalar beam weapons was being researched on the basis of Tesla technology before 1960, and by about 1968 or so, the Russians had completely developed scalar beam weapons capable of destroying anything they were aimed at. The so-called "cold war" between the Americans and Russians was an absolute scam. The same secret government group of banking families and powerful industrialists and their corporations, began the complete control of Russia, along with the U.S. which they already controlled. financed by the Rothschild and Rockefeller interests, and directed by MI-5 out of England). Didn't know that, did you? (Most folks don't.!)

A broader and focusable version of scalar wave / scalar beam technology was developed and eventually became what is now known as the "H.A.A.R.P. system". Its first main tower and antenna array is situated in Alaska. There is a completely coordinated and interconnected series of them in existence, presently being operated around the world, from Alaska to Australia.

Although you won't get anyone in government to admit it, the main uses of the "H.A.A.R.P. system" are for worldwide weather control, as well as to harass and possibly shoot down extraterrestrial craft, and also for large scale mind control.

As a means of weather control, it is capable of generating devastating hurricanes, powerful windstorms, and torrential rainstorms. It can also be used to move extremely cold air masses from the polar regions of Canada and Siberia, and relocate them into more southern areas of the northern hemisphere. That has been done many times in the past thirty years. In case congress would attempt to expose and eliminate the harp system, its operation was conveniently turned over to EXXON Corporation a few years ago. Same folks running the same show? That main corporation is EXXON in the U.S., and ESSO in Canada. (Rockefeller family !!!)

Although almost nobody knows about it, there is a lead-lined board room in the modern high rise Esso Plaza building in Calgary. (Exxon =U.S., Esso = Canada). It was set up to accommodate secret meetings of our quiet rulers, and has been used for that purpose from time to time since its completion. The author has met one of the individuals who were involved in installing that lead liner.

A Surprising number of ordinary American citizens are dumb as a fencepost when it comes to knowledge of or about Canada. That has been deliberately done by your controllers. Much of Canada is more modern than the U.S. in terms of cities and many other things, and the Canadian education system was bastardized later than yours, so many of our professionals were better prepared than yours in certain areas. We are all the same human beings to begin with...

Ref: " Contact" newspaper (the Phoenix Journals - accessible through www.four winds10.com   Also try Tesla connections on Google, and related internet publication of scalar technology studies and revelations by Tom Bearden. Also: " Angels Do Not Play This H.A.A.R.P. " by Jean Manning & Nick Begich.

Suppressed Inventions:

In this section we will deal primarily with energy based inventions of super efficiency, as well as free energy inventions. As far as this universe is concerned, the second law of thermodynamics is bullshit, but that has been kept rather quiet for quite a long time. - Since about 1856, to be more specific.

Charles Nelson Pogue - Canada

By 1935, Charley Pogue patented his first super vaporizer carburetor. By 1936, his patents began to issue. After his best carburetor had been tested quite thoroughly in 1938, on timber trucks operating out of Fort Francis Ontario, Mr. Pogue began to deal with other interested parties. As we proceed with the story, bothersome tests took place after that, and were reported in the Winnipeg Free Press. The scared controllers of the energy industry (Rockefeller, in particular) made sure this invention was thoroughly hidden and suppressed by 1940.

The author, in 1978, finally obtained copies of Pogue's two carburetor patents. They were not in the regular files in the U.S. patent office. However, a smart searcher in Washington did manage to get hold of permanently archived copies. The second improved version was a most interesting device, having two chambers in series heated by engine cooling water; with each containing a spiral wound continuous containment wall or baffle, spreading the vaporizing fuel over an expanding heat transferring surface area. Vaporizing gasoline at higher pressure, after spiraling to the centre of this first chamber, was transferred to the centre of chamber 2, and then spiraled outward to an ejection tube connected to the intake manifold. This vaporized gasoline then encountered a much higher vacuum effect in the intake, seriously reducing its pressure once again, which avoided any potential for condensation prior to ignition. The result was near total combustion. (**However, that was different gasoline...**)

The best we can expect from present "fuel injection" systems does not exceed 16% by very much. Present systems deliberately do not vaporize any measurable amount of the gasoline. Droplets do not burn, and there is no longer any means for vaporization in any of those systems. Present gasoline has been deliberately bastardized, so that it won't properly vaporize below about 450 degrees Fahrenheit. Who did that? - The Rockefeller oil & gas empire did it, and that fact was disclosed to a trusted friend of mine by one of their retired former employees.

There is a written record of the fact that in 1939, Ford Motor Company put Pogue carburetors on three brand new Ford sedans for testing purposes. The end result of the testing sequence is that those cars averaged close to 170 miles per gallon. Later on, anecdotal information came to light, that the U.S. had used Pogue carburetors on their military tanks that were involved in the final tank battle with Rommel in North Africa. With a range of 5+ times the gas mileage, the U.S. tanks did not have to refuel, and Rommel's better tanks ended up as sitting ducks. That information has since been confirmed, as the author has read it in at least two other publications.

Further test information was published with regard to the Pogue carburetor, indicating that its use consistently resulted in extremely high gas mileage. In early 1936, T.G. Breen, president of Breen Motor Company, of Winnipeg, Manitoba, tested the Pogue carburetor on a Ford V-8 coupe, and got 26.2 miles on one Imperial pint of gasoline. You multiply that figure by 8 to get gas mileage of 209.6., on an Imperial gallon. With a smaller U.S. gallon, we are dealing with a ratio of 3.63/4.545, and we would have about 167. (This shows that the 170 figure by Ford, with new cars, on better roads, as done in the U.S., was also accurately determined)

On April 30, 1936, Ford Motor Company, Winnipeg Manitoba, tested the Pogue carburetor and was "at a loss to understand" how the carburetor got 25.7 miles on one pint of gasoline (that is approximately 205 miles per gallon). Mr. W.J. Holmes and Mr. Purdy conducted the test for Ford Motor Company.

On Dec. 12, 1936, Canadian Automotive Magazine stated that the standard carburetor gets about 25 miles per gallon at only 9% efficiency. Therefore the Pogue carburetor was 72% efficient over-all at 200+ miles per gallon. In 1953, CARS Magazine stated that in the opening months of 1936, Pogue panicked the Toronto Stock Exchange and threw fright into the major oil companies. Stock exchange offices and brokers were swamped with orders to dump all oil stock immediately. This same article stated that Winnipeg's largest automobile dealers tested the Pogue carburetor and got results of up to 216.8 miles per gallon. Why has gasoline deteriorated so much since that time???

I have direct experience with regard to "denial of approval" of my pyrolytic fuel vaporizer by the California Air Resources Board - this was in 1991, as I remember. Also the Fish / Kendig variable venturi carburetor had been turned down by the same Air Resources Board in the 1970's following it being a winner in the California Air Pollution car race. They do not seem to want "clean air", and "somebody" in the background seemed to have a powerful influence ...

As an interesting point to ponder, the author has read published material, put out in the 1980's by a Canadian inventor and researcher into energy devices. His name is George Wiseman, and he was at that time living in British Columbia. He called his little outfit "Eagle Research". He had done years of experimenting by the time he wrote his short and highly informative articles on fuel vaporization devices, and had invented a couple of his own.

He made two bothersome statements. Firstly, that only about one sixth, or less, of the gasoline was actually being effectively applied to doing any work, and that if the gasoline were efficiently applied to the job, our cars would get at least five times their best gas mileage, and the most likely potential was over seven times the mileage then obtainable with carburetors of that time. The second bothersome statement he made was that the way gasoline is currently structured in its chemical form, its "heavier ends" would not completely vaporize without boiling, and that it takes about 450 degrees F. to boil the present version of our gasoline. George is said to be a "Mensa" type with an I.Q. above 160.

Pardon me for rambling here, but I have been exposed to such diverse sources of information that the real truth tends to eventually become apparent. For example, I have a friend in Edmonton, who has been dealing with energy devices for an American inventor and businessman, by the name of Dennis Lee. My friend, Ken Nelson, coincidentally ended up on a flight out of Denver one day, sitting next to a retired chemical engineer from a Rockefeller controlled oil and gas company. When he asked the engineer what had been going on to do with the subject of carburetion and fuel vaporization, he got a surprise.

The engineer said that his specialty was changing the nature of gasoline so that it would not effectively vaporize in any of those super efficiency carburetors, and he had been employed at doing just that for more than 25 years. Sometimes seemingly random information from two or three odd sources can lead to answers to some of the most bothersome questions... There we go... Mushroomed again!!

Ref: http://eagle-research.com

It is also a good source Re: Brown's Gas & other energy-related devices and inventions. The author is aware of other 3 or 4 high efficiency carburetors, including the Fish / Kendig variable venturi model which was made in California in the 1950's. A carburetor invented by Johnny Heddy was also taken off the market by being bought out by a consortium of smaller oil companies, back in Oklahoma, in 1939. However none of those stories compare to the saga of Charles Nelson Pogue.

The author, and at least two others he is aware of, including Mr. Wiseman, have invented pyrolytic gasoline vaporizers that vaporize gasoline, without oxidation, at very high temperatures. The author has put his in a drawer, for the sake of his own safety, and doesn't know what the other inventors might have experienced in the meantime... In a somewhat different direction, we will get into hydrogen generators and water burners and splitters as we move forward and deal with the potentials for replacement of hydrocarbon fuels....

Breaking News - Jan.30/08 -A Brown's Gas generator module system, promising up to 100% gas mileage improvement has now been presented on my favorite "fully truthful website". This little unit is simple, compact and easy to install. It is now beginning to look like the good changes will come in spite of our government systems and fully controlled and lying media.

Dr. Sam Leach - U.S.A.

Dr. Sam Leach was one of the most brilliant and prolific inventors that the author has ever met, and became familiar with. Among his more than 140 patented inventions is a system which splits water into Hydrogen and Oxygen, and feeds it into the intake of an automobile engine. The end result is that water comes out the tailpipe as the system powers the automobile rather efficiently. That invention was covered in an old issue of Motor Trend Magazine 1988 or 1989, as I remember the situation. (Sam had a doctorate in Physics plus a degree in Aeronautical Engineering and a major in Optics.)

Dr. Leach's other suppressed inventions are:
1. A sheet type of fluorescent lighting system, which would light up the entire wall, or any surface area covered by the plastic sheeting that emitted the light. That one was presented to Sylvania in the early 1980's, and Sam could not raise any money for further development after that point in time. His system was 46% more efficient than any other existing fluorescent lighting technology.

2. Plasma Power. Dr. Leach had patented a plasma power system, which like then existing systems of Westinghouse and G.E., burns water at very high temperatures, beyond 25,000 degrees F. The big difference was that Dr. Leach's system, after extensive testing achieved higher temperatures and proved to be over one hundred and fifty percent efficient.

Westinghouse and G.E. systems were capable of generating maximum temperatures in the order of 35,000 degrees F, and Dr. Leach's system could reach temperatures beyond 60,000 degrees F. Why the difference? There are a couple of reasons, including making the water conductive, but the main one is that Dr. Leach's system generates fusion energy from plain water, and nobody has ever been told anything about that, inside or outside of our schools.

The author assisted Dr. Leach with his business plan, and spent a great deal of time and effort toward securing financing for further development and deployment. To make a long story short, there was no way anyone amongst the wealthiest of companies, supposedly with the most to gain, would put up a dime. Dr. Leach had confirmed that his system was capable of generating electricity by means of steam turbines in 1988, at a base cost of less than one third of a cent per kilowatt.

Water power could not even touch that system!!

When the author was dealing with Dr. Leach in 1993, he said that strange things were going on to do with his plasma power invention, and any efforts to get the system financed. Since Dr. Sam had an I.Q. of 200, he did not miss much, so when his car had been bugged, he removed the bug and waited for the next happening which could be related. Not long after he disposed of the bug, he got a threatening phone call. Being much smarter than the average cat, he hung up on the caller after hearing what he had to say, immediately dialed the telephone operator, and asked for a reconnection.

When he was reconnected, the Mossad Office answered his call. Perhaps that would lead you to wonder what the real background connections might have been, and how come the Mossad were then involved? - and why in hell is the Mossad prying into the private lives of any Americans, and who is in control in the U.S.??? It sure as hell doesn't appear to be congress or the senate or the elected representatives of ordinary citizens. (Remember Khazarians?)

Mushroomed again on at least three fronts, including one that appears to be related to government. Whose government?? Who really controls America?? Hold onto that one. When I get into who's who, more completely, that will be rather apparent, in spite of what you see and hear on your controlled media.

Ref: Direct personal experience only. There are no other written references to Dr. Leach that the author is presently aware of.

Louis Szabo - Canada

Louis, a Hungarian immigrant to Canada, is being mentioned and covered here, as he is another one of the oddly unique and brilliant inventors I have met. By and large, he is known for his invention of certain fittings and accessories which relate to electrical power transmission and distribution lines.

In our discussions he explained that he had been trained as an electrical and electronics engineer in Hungary. Back in 1958, at the time of the Hungarian revolution, as it has been called, Louis quietly escaped from Hungary, and eventually ended up in the Vancouver area of British Columbia.

The odd thing about Mr. Szabo's situation was (in 1983-84) that he only had to pay B.C. Hydro for electrical energy consumed in his front office, and he did not pay a nickel for the energy consumed in his fair sized shop, which had two lathes and other normal pieces of shop equipment. Because we were both free-thinking conceptual inventors, we got along rather well, and he eventually wanted to show me confidentially how he achieved his free energy arrangement in the shop. (As I remember, he showed me the system in about 1987.)

When Louis took me back into his shop, he showed me a vintage 1949 squirrel cage 3-phase 230 volt electrical generator, rated at about 25 kilowatts. At the drive pulley end of the generator, there was a loose V-belt resting on the drive pulley, and the other end was loosely over the output pulley of a 1 horsepower electric motor. It is to be noted here, that since we were dealing with an induction generator, unless its output wires were connected to a load, it would almost free wheel, with very little resistance against the power to turn it at rather high speed, so a 1 HP motor was adequate to bring it up to 1725 RPM with no load.

The electric motor was mounted on a properly shaped piece of ¾" plywood hinged at the opposite end of the board from the motor. A large diameter coil spring was holding the motor mount end of the board upward in suspension, so the drive belt was quite loose.

A bundle of taped up wires was coming out of the generator, and connected to a "black box", with a push button switch on the front. (black boxes are things of great interest, and to most people they are really supposed to be mysterious…) The next happenings were absolutely fascinating. Louis walked up to the generator, and said "are you ready"?, and I said Yessir, let's go!

He plugged in the 1 HP electric motor, ran it up to speed, and gradually depressed the spring loaded board, achieving clutch effect with the belt, and soon the motor had brought the generator up to its normal operating speed of 1,725 +- R.P.M. Then he pushed the control button on the black box, and suddenly, a powerful humming sound cut in. He then backed off on the spring loaded board, pulled off the belt, and hung it on a nail on the wall. The generator was humming along, and putting out approximately 10 kilowatts...

Then, with a twinkle in his eye, he asked me if I had any idea how he was achieving that result... Being in my own element as a free-thinker and fellow inventor, I suggested to him that there may be 9 segments in that generator. He confirmed that was true. I then said that his cute little black box was set up so that he had 6 segments driving, and 3 segments putting out, and he said that was really the case... I did not ask him any more questions, as he had already decided years before, that revealing anything about his invention being a free energy device would lead to dire consequences. After years of oppression in a communist country, he did not trust our system of things either.

That was one of the very simple ways to generate free power. There are other ways, known to me and a serious number of other inventors at the present time. I will now predict that solid state free energy generators like the so-called zero point energy generator that was patented in the U.S. on March 26th., 2003, which has been kept rather quiet since that time, will become common means to that end in the near future. There will be more of them in a number of different configurations, and we will begin to see them rather soon. There have been individuals and groups throughout history who have held the monopoly on money, but none of those folks have any monopoly on intelligence and creativity.

Ref: Direct personal experience only. Virtually nobody else knows about Mr. Szabo's system of things, and I am not about to expose him any further, in spite of the fact that other inventors including myself, have invented free energy electrical generators of different configurations.. There will come a time to bring those new generators out, and it is not the right time at the present moment. That time will come after the truth is out, and our Illuminati-based corporate fascist governments are replaced.

A Mushroom Wakeup Call:
In a very lengthy article concerning suppressed energy inventions, published on the internet in the fall of 2006, Gary Vesperman presented suppression case statistics. I have no reason to doubt the number, quality or veracity of his sources, and here is the information he had compiled at that time:

Number of Energy Invention Suppression Incidents = 53
Number of dead, missing or injured energy
    inventors & associates = 13
Number of energy inventors threatened with death = 16
Number of energy researchers and associates
    imprisoned = 7
Number of incidents involving the CIA = 4
Number of incidents involving the U.S. gov't = 27
Number of inventions classified as secret
    by the U. S. Patent Office = 4,000

It is unfortunate that most people in North America and the rest of the world are seriously unaware of the amount of suppression that has been going on. The main reason for this is that the same group of money and corporate controllers had already achieved virtually total control of all of the media in the U.S., and to a great extent in most other countries as early as 1954. You will note that in my source references, I have mentioned Gary Vesperman's work. He has done a very good 40 page article on suppressed new energy inventions, and **www.rense.com** has published it for a very large audience on their very popular website.

How in hell were you going to be able to read the truth if none of the major media was prepared to publish it? - Who actually owns the major media? It is none other than the group of banking families and interrelated industrial and media corporations that have key persons on the controlling boards of directors of all of those institutions. They call the shots, based on their own agendas. Their main agenda is the matter of controlling all of the world's population by controlling all of the money and sources of energy, food, and news and Information. If anyone assumes that does not mean controlling government, they are not only a mushroom, but could be mentally "challenged"?, as well.

Congress in the U.S. has been almost totally bought and paid for, and its general performance must conform toward achieving the end result envisioned by their Controllers. The same probably applies in the other closely connected countries like Canada. Americans are more inclined to stand up and raise hell from time to time, so we can observe more easily what is happening in the U.S. from day to day. However, I am sure the same is true in Canada, England, and most others in the G8 group of countries, and to a great extent in most countries outside of this major group as well. From individually uninformed perspectives, we who are outside of the U.S. could be more mushroomed than the Americans.

The internet became part of our normal scenario many years ago, and largely maintained its integrity as a system of things in the communications business. If that had not happened, most of us who have some understanding of what has been going on would be isolated as objecting individuals, and nobody would get to know we even exist.

To fill you in a little further:
I could continue this process of identifying and explaining suppressed inventions until we have hundreds of pages for you to read, and I want you to realize that there are many very

intelligent and highly creative individuals in the U.S. and Canada. There may be lower proportions in Europe, but there are many free-thinking individuals there as well, who have retained their keen intellect and creativity in spite of the more restrictive government systems in place in Europe.

I am now going to give you an idea of how sharp some of those creative people are, and this example is from the U.S. Gary Vesperman had published this series of comments from an inventor, and I picked it up on his earlier mentioned article as published on the **rense.com** website.

This is what a now retired inventor had to say - - -
"I had an electronics business down in south Florida where I owned and sponsored a small boat race team through my business, starting in 1988. We had a machine shop out back of my business for doing engine work, and I worked on engines for other racers and a local mini-sub research outfit that was building surface running drone type boats for the DEA. I delved into hydrogen research where I was building small electrolyzer type units that used distilled water mixed with an electrolyte and I would resonate the plates for optimal conversion efficiency".

"I discovered that with the right frequencies, I was able to generate monatomic hydrogen and oxygen, which when recombined, produces about 4 times the energy of normal diatomic hydrogen and oxygen molecules since the process of combustion does not have to break apart the molecules first before recombining into water vapor. Diatomic hydrogen requires about 4% to air to produce the same power as gasoline, while monatomic requires slightly less than 1% to air for the same power".

"The only drawback was that storage at pressure causes the monatoms to start joining into diatomic pairs, and the mixture weakens, so it must be produced on-demand and consumed right away. I used modified LP carburetors on the boat engines to deal with using vapor fuel. I even converted an old

Chrysler with a slant six engine to run on the hydrogen setup and we tested it in the shop".

"I never published anything of what I was working on, and we always stated that our boats were running on hydrogen fuel, which was allowed, to avoid any controversy at the races. It was not until many years later that I found out what I had stumbled upon was already discovered and known as "Brown's Gas", and there were companies out there selling equipment and plans to make it".

"I had never tried to market anything, but was plagued with trouble ever since I did the conversion to the old Chrysler and did a few test runs on it in the shop. My shop, which had never had any major crime problems before, suddenly was getting broken into, and pieces of equipment related to the hydrogen project were getting vandalized or stolen. I thought it might be that one of the guys that worked for me might have leaked something to someone and they were trying to either steal the technology or stop me from working on it. I ended up shutting down the research, getting out of it all, converting the engines back to racing fuel and selling off the racing boats. The break-ins stopped, and I had no further trouble from that time. I totally closed the business and retired in 1991".

The above example is only one of many, where the usual B.S. we are taught in our schools is proven to be only just that. There is over unity. There is free and abundant energy. The entire universe is free energy in motion. This business of being treated like a mushroom is real, and it has been happening all along to all of us within the system that has been controlling all of us, dumbing us down, and keeping us ignorant for many generations. Any time one of us gets to the point in our research where we have a way of producing and using free energy, and the controlling folks at the top or their bird dogs find out about it, we are subjected to everything from harassment to assassination, and that is a fact.

Murder & Attempted Murder:

Dr. Henry T. Moray - U.S.A.

There has been a great deal written about Dr. Moray, and he had given a rather large number of public demonstrations of his solid state electrical output system. I cannot call it a generating system, because all it did was pull in energy from the aetheric matrix (all of surrounding space), and with his system grounded, a great deal of electrical energy output began to flow. Those demonstrations began in 1938 or earlier, and Moray was becoming well known by the local electrical utilities, etc.

In 1940, Henry T. Moray demonstrated before the members of the Public Utilities Commission in Utah. His free energy generator gave a continuous output of 250,000 volts with no apparent input. The next day he was found shot in his lab and all of his notes and his device had been stolen.

Ref: Vassilatos, Vesperman and earlier authors - try Google to expand your range of sources concerning Dr. Moray. Also, Vesperman's material came from www.rense.com .

Floyd Sweet - U.S.A.

Floyd Sweet was a very active and gifted researcher into the matters of higher group symmetry electrodynamics, and had come up with a tremendously powerful vacuum triode amplifier. This was leading to the further development of drastically extended electromagnetic technology, with a number of new phenomena, including means to control, and the demonstrated potential of neutralizing or seriously suppressing the effects of gravity.

In an experiment set up by Tom Bearden (later involved in the zero point generator technology and patent), and carried out by Sweet, the weight of an object was steadily reduced by 90% on the laboratory bench. Apparently this information got out, and the wrong people found out about it.

Sweet was fired at from a point about 300 yards away by a would-be-assassin, using a silenced rifle. Sweet had stumbled and fallen down on the steps just as the assassin pulled the trigger. The bullet snapped right by his ear, where his head had just been. Sweet then became quite paranoid about continuing development of his technology.

According to Tom Bearden, Sweet received death threats over the phone and some threats face to face. One direct incident was where a well-dressed man walked up to Sweet, told him he represented a conglomerate that did not want Sweet's device to appear in the world at this time, and that unfortunate things can happen to people who do not comply with the wishes of others.

John Andrews - Portugal

John Andrews was a Portuguese chemist. He demonstrated a water to gas additive before U.S. Navy officials which allowed ordinary water to be added to gasoline without decreasing the combustibility of the gas. It is also suggested that at the time it could possibly have reduced the net cost of gasoline to as little as two cents per gallon. This is another case where the wrong people found out about it, and took immediate action. When Navy officials went to Mr. Andrews lab to negotiate for the formula, they found Andrews missing, and his lab ransacked.

Ref: Gary Vesperman - for this one and others previously listed above.

Dennis Lee - U.S.A.

In the 1980's Dennis Lee invented a freon-based low-temperature phase-change engine which could have been a follow-up to the Sterling engine, and in more recent terms, another more efficient heat engine by Bob Stewart of the U.S.

A small plant was set up in the Seattle area to produce a commercial home-scale electrical generator system, utilizing the Dennis Lee engine as its power plant. A Seattle area power company campaigned to shut down the plant. According to Gary Vesperman, <u>even a female employee was murdered</u>.

Dennis was forced to move his company to southern California, and start over. He was shortly thereafter <u>imprisoned on a false charge for two years</u>. His book."The Alternative" documents the falsity of the charge.

He made the claim that freon has been scientifically determined to be not destructive of the earth's atmospheric ozone layer. **(he is correct in that case)** He said that the secret group which had been suppressing certain clean energy inventions is so afraid of his invention that they had cleverly arranged a ban on freon refrigerant in air conditioners etc. in order to stop him. **(that is also correct.),** and the same controlling group also changed from lead as an "anti-knock" compound in gasoline (it was put there to ruin the super carburetors) to bromine which is an extremely bad compound in gaseous form as a dangerous element when exposed to the ozone layer. (The bad boys don't give a rat's ass about the environment, and total control and the maximizing of income from the energy business are far more important to them than the environment.)

As further comments with regard to suppressed inventions, before we get into the matter of the "One World Order" group of money and power grabbing egotistical idiots, who are motivated through secret societies etc., I will now mention some of those other suppressed inventions as a closing presentation in this chapter.

1.)   A system for totally energizing water, leading to the precipitation of any unnatural elements in the water, and making the water pure, fresh and highly energized. This discovery has been thoroughly checked out by the U.S. secret government, and has been put into abeyance, as it does not fit into their present agenda, in spite of the fact that it could clean up the oceans seas and lakes on this beautiful planet in as little as two years.

Ref: www.fourwinds10.com - Drunvaldo Melchizedek

2.)   A system for totally neutralizing atomic radiation. Because our present controllers control us through fear and intimidation, they decided that system must not come forward until "they" decide to do that. In the meantime, they have been progressively murdering U.S. soldiers and the citizens of Iraq, through their use of depleted uranium, as smeared onto their ammunition, etc... Vesperman's report includes one likely case of assassination of an inventor who came up with a way to neutralize atomic radiation.

Ref: garyvesperman@yahoo.com   (History of "New Energy" Invention Suppression Cases) Gary has done much work on the situation. His very good article also references other sources to keep you moving forward...

3.)   Anti Gravity drive systems as invented and perfected by Thomas Townsend Brown back in the 1960's. (Our controllers had recovered such technology from crashed extra-terrestrial craft and had back-engineered it successfully before 1960) However, to avoid the possibility of Brown's technology getting into the hands of some uncontrolled private outfit, Mr. Brown was quietly and carefully removed from the sequence of things. He eventually retired, virtually broke, and no longer capable of pursuing further development of his technology.

4.)   Fusion energy generation as perfected and completely demonstrated by Filo Farnsworth in 1965, and that system could have continued from that time to generate electricity for all of the U.S. and anywhere else at less than one cent per kilowatt. That technology was bought out and tied up for a period of 30 years by ITT in the U.S., which was already majority owned by Krupp in Germany, by about 1937 - Krupp ties back to the original Illuminati banking families.

Ref: Lost Science - by Gerry Vassilatos

5.)   A cure for cancer, based on frequency, effective within a radius of miles, as developed and demonstrated by Royal Rife, of California, as early as 1938. Cancer by that time was a 20 billion dollar industry in the U.S., and curing cancer was never the objective of the cancer society or the medical establishment.

In the early 1920's, Dr. Otto Warburg in Germany had proven that he could cause cancer to occur. He could also quickly eliminate the problem, by changing the Ph level in the body, & opening up the cell's ability to absorb oxygen. Cancer action involves CO_2 metabolism (Anaerobic). All of this is known information, if you can find it, bearing in mind that the same group of criminals controls the media, and the American Cancer Society, and won't publish anything that might interfere with their long term objective of total enslavement of the population.

In the 20's, cancer was a $19B industry. The American Cancer Society was the organization that sunk Mr. Rife, and eventually turned him into a broken man. The best of his technology had to be secretly removed to Mexico to avoid its seizure and destruction. Since that time, the Rife technology and related frequency devices have been recreated in the U.S. and in Canada. I am presently aware that such technology is now being used and applied in Calgary and Edmonton. A missing element of the Rife technology is a 17,000 power purely optical microscope which allowed the viewer to see all bacteria and viruses, and observe when the frequency would destroy the bacteria or virus involved, including the "BX" and "BY" cancer viruses. The cancer viruses were clearly seen, named and photographed by Dr. Rife. His 17,000 power optical microscope has not been equaled since his time.

The establishment wanted people to believe that there was no such thing as a cancer virus. They have been deliberately pushing electron microscopes in the meantime. Also, our academic institutions don't know much if anything about the superior Rife optical microscope technology.

Electron microscopes tend to destroy bacteria and viruses to begin with, so they cannot be clearly observed with an electron microscope. - Cancer was already a multi-billion dollar industry in 1925, and its gross value to the establishment has greatly increased since then. Seems to be the reason for the present situation.

Radiation treatment increases the activity of both the BX and BY cancer viruses, and chemotherapy for the most part, has an absolutely dismal record toward any potential for curing cancer. Do you expect that the establishment would tell you that? - Not very likely...

Ref: "The Cancer Cure That Worked", and "The Cancer Conspiracy" - by Barry Lynes.

Chapter 2

MEDICINE: THE BEST CURES ARE BEING SUPPRESSED BY THE PHARMACEUTICAL COMPANIES, AND THEY ALSO CONTROL THE MEDICAL SCHOOLS

Super bacteria & virus killers have been suppressed mostly since about 1910, when the Rockefeller business empire began to take a dominant position in the pharmaceutical and drug industry. This will be an eye-opener for most people.

Lugol's Solution - This is a colloidal suspension, where the human body will use what it needs, and reject the remainder of the fluid product. With that obviously French name, it was created in France a very long time ago, not too far from the time of Pasteur. In any case, Lugol's Solution is a very powerful anti-bacterial, and can stop a serious number of the most common bacterial infections. Among them is the entire range of herpes bacteria, including the common cold, cold sores and the flu.

It is of further interest to note that Lugol's will eliminate Salmonella and Shigella, the most common food poisoning bacteria in little more than an hour, if you were to take it soon enough. I have personally and quickly zeroed out salmonella in as little as 1 hour, and have cured my wife of the same potential problem, with the early application of Lugol's. Lugol's is also effective against tonsillitis, and will eliminate the necessity for a tonsillectomy, as I have personally proven, after a 30 year series of bouts of tonsillitis and many doctors recommending the removal of my tonsils.

Lugol's also works very quickly and efficiently to eliminate the bacteria responsible for Hydrophobia, also referred to as Rabies. The main reason why Lugol's works as well as an anti-bacterial is that when you take a dose, it lodges in the tonsils and lymph glands & spleen, through which all of the body's blood supply must flow. As your blood passes through those marvelous organs, the Lugol's solution nails the bacteria and viruses, and your apparent problem is seriously reduced rather quickly. That is bearing in mind that the body has to get rid of the dead viruses and bacteria, and that takes some time. In most cases, the mainly fungus-based drugs referred to as antibiotics are far less effective. Antibiotics make one hell of a lot of money for the pharmaceutical companies. However, the main side effect of antibiotics is candida, which is a virulent fungus infection in the human body, and very difficult to eradicate, to the point where millions of people, (women in particular) have to tolerate its effects for the remainder of their lifetimes.

The author has been using Lugol's for about 35 years, with excellent results most of the time, and would suggest that the reader consider it on their own responsibility for colds, flu, and a serious number of other common ailments. The reason why I am suggesting your own responsibility, is that present regulations would make me responsible for screw-ups and consequences if you had a bad reaction (almost impossible), or took too much, (60+ drops when a normal dose in water would be 6 to 9 drops). In any event, Lugol's is a good replacement for a large number of potentially damaging pharmaceutical remedies. You might take a look at it, to have a simple off the shelf remedy, rather than paying a ridiculous amount of money for a product provided by the pharmaceutical companies which is usually damaging to your body, even in the short term.

Ref: Folk Medicine - by Dr. Jarvis - Also, to get the product, in the Calgary area, we can buy prepared bottles (200 ml.) of Lugol's from Shoppers Drug Mart in particular, but if you were to ask the pharmacist in any case, they can order it as a standard item from their supplier in Vancouver, B.C...You will have to ask your pharmacist at your local drug store in the U.S. The Pharmacist can make it up, as the formula is well known, or there may by now be a normal source in the U.S. - Check it out. In Canada, I can buy 200 ml. at a local price ranging from $7.95 to $9.00. When compared to a pharmaceutical product, that is a rather good deal, for at least a two year supply of Lugol's Solution.

A very important article on Silver Colloid, presented on the website fourwinds10.com by Patrick H. Bellringer - reprinted from 2003

Before I proceed, it is pertinent that this is the most complete and totally revealing of at least 4 well-written articles I have read on Silver Colloid over the last 20 years or so.. Everything else, as I proceed is word for word by P.H.B.

Colloidal Silver (CS) is a natural antibiotic which has been used throughout the world for centuries as a means to destroy microbes of all kinds and to correct many health problems. It was removed from public use in the United States in the 1920's and 1930's by the medical profession in their move to purge natural health remedies from the marketplace. As late as August 1998 the FDA ordered all colloidal silver removed from all U.S. Health Stores, but due to public outcry, that order has been temporarily relaxed. Today, the use of colloidal silver is spreading rapidly throughout the medical community in the healing of burn victims. Medical doctors have never denied the merits of silver in the form of silver nitrate as a bactericide. Silver nitrate is routinely used in drops put into a baby's eyes at birth to prevent blindness from venereal disease.

Silver acts as a second immune system for humans by destroying bacteria and viruses of all kinds. It is toxic to bacteria, viruses, yeasts, fungi, (molds), protozoa, and parasites in the egg stage. Therefore CS will destroy staph and strep bacteria which are so common in today's health problems. In the silver literature there are listings of over 650 diseases and health problems that silver in colloidal form will affect in very positive ways. The frequency of silver is higher than almost all of the known harmful crystal-headed viruses such as AIDS, Ebola, West Nile, and SARS and thus will destroy them. Usually those viruses are no problem to a person with a strong immune system and good nutrition.

Those dying from such diseases today usually have neither.

A colloidal is a substance of ultramicroscopic particles. Colloidal Silver is nothing more than very tiny particles of pure silver suspended in distilled water through the process of electrolysis. The smaller the particles on CS the better the body can assimilate them. Colloidal silver is odorless, tasteless and has no known negative reaction to any medication, health problem, diet or artificial alteration to the human body. It is considered, along with Gold and Titanium to be God's natural antibiotic, provided for the health of the people of planet Earth. Gold has a higher frequency than silver, while the frequency of titanium is higher than gold. Nothing on Earth in microbe form can survive the frequencies of colloidal titanium and colloidal gold, while colloidal silver will destroy nearly all of them.

Dr. Hulda Regehr Clark has done extensive research and application in the field of holistic health. She has published her works in various books and newsletters. For further information on colloidal silver, I am drawing from an edited copy of one of Dr. Clark's newsletters on the subject. "What do you know about colloidal silver?" Edited by: Christine Doyle. From Dr. Clark's newsletter: http:www.silverpuppy. com/drclarknews.html

This article was taken, shortened and altered, from Dr. Clark's Newsletter for practitioners, "Finding the Way", by courtesy of the editor, clinical and Nutritionist practitioner, Christine Doyle, PO Box 33, Carmarthen SA33 6YE, UK, Tel/Fax +44-1994-484-682.

A 1994 issue of "Newsweek" featured a 6-page article, "Antibiotics, The End of Miracle Drugs?" as the cover story. "The rise of drug-resistant germs is unparalleled in recorded history", according to the article. "Penicillin and tetracycline lost their power over staph back in the 1950's and 60's. Another antibiotic, Methicillin, provided a backup for a while, but Methicillin-resistant staph is now common in hospitals and nursing homes worldwide. Trying to cripple bacteria's defences will not do much more than buy us five to ten years. A better strategy might be to abandon antibiotics altogether in favour of different kinds of drugs." Not a very pretty picture: bacteria have a tremendous ability to adapt to substances. They can and do mutate to overcome antibiotics. When the antibiotics destroy the bacteria which are susceptible to them, they can clear the way for resistant bacteria to move in uninhibited.

Still another problem that has plagued the medical profession from the beginning with modern antibiotics has been that beneficial bacteria and organisms play various important, natural functions in the body. Antibiotics often play havoc with some of the friendly organisms, producing long lasting side effects that may be difficult to correct.

One reason that antibiotics have been so popular in the medical field is due to the fact that they can be patented. Also, pharmaceutical companies find it financially worthwhile to keep the doctors educated in their medicines, while other products go unnoticed. Silver, on the other hand, is not patentable and there are no huge profits in it, so it is not worth heavy promotion. The high-priced products run over the low cost products, simply because of profitability. All of this is happening at the same time that disease bacteria are developing immunity to antibiotics all over the world. The medical profession is alarmed.

Science Digest suggested an answer to all of these catastrophic problems back in March of 1978, in an article titled "Our Mightiest germ Fighter". This article by Jim Powell stated: "Thanks to eye-opening research, silver is emerging as a wonder of modern medicine. "An antibiotic kills perhaps a half-dozen different disease organisms, but silver kills some 650. Resistant strains fail to develop. Moreover, silver is virtually non-toxic."

Silver has been known to be a bactericide for at least 1200

years. Even in ancient times, it was known to prevent disease, and it was said that disease could not be transmitted in drinking from a silver cup. Silver coins were commonly dropped into a jar to prevent the spoilage of milk and other drink, and silver containers were used to prolong the freshness of foods in general. Wealthy people used to feed their babies with a silver spoon, which was considered to be a cause of strong healthy growth. Even today, some commonly call all tableware "silverware" although it is more commonly stainless steel. In the 1920's, 30's and 40's, silver was ground very fine like flour, suspended in water and was used orally for many infections and disease conditions, topically on burns, and for fungal infections. Until almost 1970 it was common for scientists to put a silver dime in a petri dish to sterilize the dish. Silver was long used for plates for the surgical repair of bones. After the development of the patented antibiotics, silver was forgotten in the United States and most other places, although antibiotics are only effective against bacteria, not viruses, yeast, or fungi. Now, with the greatly improved modern colloids, the tables are turning and silver may be the most effective treatment of all.

What exactly is colloidal silver (CS)?

Simply put, colloids are extremely minute silver particles suspended in water, with a positive electrical charge. The smaller the silver particles the more effective CS has proven to be. The best Colloidal Silver is produced at the molecular level. A small DC current is passed through an electrolyte (distilled water) with silver electrodes. Minute molecular sized particles are drawn off the positive electrode, having a positive electrical charge. This electrical charge is of primary importance to healing and antibacterial qualities. The charge slowly dissipates, especially when exposed to light, and therefore, the freshness of the colloid is important.

In "Colloidal Silver", a booklet produced by the Association for Colloidal Research, it is reported that: "Medical journal reports and documented studies spanning 100 years indicate no known side effects from oral or IV administration of properly manufactured colloidal silver in animal or human testing. There has never been a reported reaction with Colloidal Silver to any prescription medication."

The evidence appears to support the theory that Colloidal Silver is highly effective against all strains of pathogenic bacteria, while any one antibiotic is only effective against a few certain bacterial strains. Furthermore, antibiotics have never been effective against viruses, yeast or fungi. Yet, researchers are telling us that Colloidal Silver has produced phenomenal results in tissue healing and reconstruction, as well as reducing scar tissue in clinical tests. Severe cuts and wounds have healed in much less time. Laboratory tests have shown CS to kill over 650 destructive bacteria, viruses and fungi within 6 minutes of contact.

UCLA ran some tests on Colloidal Silver and their report states: "The silver solutions were antibacterial for streptococcus pyogenes, Staphylococcus aurous, Neisseria gonorrhea, Gardnerella vaginalis, Salmonella Typhi, and other enteric pathogens, fungicidal for Candida albicans, Candida globate, and M. furfur, and it killed every virus that we tested in the lab.

Other Voices:

Dr. Hirschberg, Johns Hopkins ". remarkable for their beneficial action in infective states". Dr. Henry Cooks: I know of no microbe that is not killed in laboratory tests within minutes". Dr. Gary Smith: "When silver was present the cancer cell was differentiated and the body was restored".

Certain bacteria are essential to healthy body function. Several researchers claim Colloidal Silver only attacks the unfriendly pathogens and will not harm the friendly ones, but one must wonder how it can possibly differentiate. The explanation is that the friendly bacteria are aerobic, while unfriendly bacteria are anaerobic. Silver does not attack bacteria directly, but rather decomposes certain enzymes the anaerobic bacteria, viruses, yeast, and mould require. The silver acts as a catalyst and is not consumed in the process. It is probable that this indirect action is also the reason bacteria cannot develop a resistance to silver, as they do to antibiotics.

Some researchers do tell us, however, that in prolonged, very heavy doses, some silver compounds will leave grey deposits in the heavier skin folds such as the knuckles. This condition is known as "Argyria". The only problem to these deposits is said to be the cosmetic appearance and the condition is said to be rare. Some experts say this condition has never been known to occur from silver in the colloidal state. Other experts do however, warn that this might be a problem with extremely high prolonged dosages (such as drinking many quarts of CS per day over months of time). The very small particle size in the Colloidal Silver would seem to make this possibility remote. Argyria is correctable with laser treatment, like a tattoo. (It should be noted that there has been only one case of argyria in the world in the last 100 years.)

Medical Uses:

In the 1970's Dr. Carl Moyer, chairman of Washington University's Department of Surgery, received a grant to develop better treatments for burn victims. Dr. Harry Margraf worked with Dr. Moyer and other surgeons, a chief biochemist on this project. They tested 22 antiseptic compounds and rejected all of them. The problem was that infections in burns often failed to respond to antibiotics. Most antiseptics actually destroy the delicate healing tissues in severe burns and were very painful. The greatest problem was the bacterium Pseudomonas acrogenous, which is particularly infectious to burns and fails to respond to all common antibiotics.

In his research into medical history, Dr. Margraf found numerous references to silver as an anti-microbial agent. Dr. Margraf therefore, tried silver nitrate, the same solution sided in newborn babies' eyes at birth to prevent blindness from venereal disease. It worked! However, he found it disturbed the balance of body salts, stained everything it touched, and in high concentrations, was corrosive and painful. After further study he found that all of those problems were solved by Colloidal Silver. With Colloidal Silver as the base, he then developed a salve that has been extremely effective in treating the infections and healing in serious burns. Colloidal Silver is now routinely used for severe burn victims, resulting in a large reduction of scarring and a heavy reduction of deaths for extensive severe burns.

The article in Science Digest, March 1978, relates: "A speeding car overturned and burst into flames. The 18 year old driver suffered burns all over his face, neck arms, back stomach and legs. Burns covered more than 80 percent of the body. Until recently, this would have been a death sentence. Doctors knew how to restore vital body fluids and salts, but had no way to fight infection, the primary cause of death in burn cases. Fortunately for this youth, a new silver compound killed deadly bacteria and enabled him to heal. He was out of the hospital within four months."

Another line of research that has led to this change of thinking is described in the best seller "The Body Electric", in which Robert O. Becker, leading research scientist in the field of bone regeneration, states: "The germ killing action of silver has been known for some time. The Soviets use silver ions to sterilize recycled water aboard their space stations. It kills even the antibiotic-resistant strains, and also works on fungus infections." He goes on to say: "It stimulates bone-forming cells, cures the most common stubborn infections of all kinds of bacteria, and stimulates healing in the skin and other soft tissues."

Certainly that is a broad statement, but Dr. Becker further relates a fascinating story which would seem to substantiate his belief. A man's broken right tibia and fibula refused to bond and the skin refused to heal over a large area of the leg for a year and a half. The leg was infected with five kinds of bacteria, all of which refused to respond to antibiotics. As a last resort before amputation, Dr. Becker treated the condition with silver charged with a very minute electrical current. This produced silver ions in the bone area and at the surface area. "I derided (cleaned) the wound, removing the dead tissue and all grossly infected or dead bone. There wasn't much left afterward. It was an enormous excavation running almost from his knee to his ankle. In the operating room, we soaked a big piece of silver nylon in saline solution and laid it over the wound. We packed the fabric in place with saline-soaked gauze, wrapped the leg, and connected the battery unit."

"About two weeks later", Dr. Becker tells us, "all of our bacterial cultures were sterile - all five kinds had been killed. The soft healing tissue, called granulation tissue, was spreading out and covering the bone. In two weeks the whole base of the wound, which had been over 8 square inches of raw bone, was covered with this friendly pink carpet. The skin was beginning to grow in too, so we could forget about the grafts we thought we needed to do. I decided to take an x-ray to see how much bone he'd lost." He was expecting the bone to start withdrawing before the knitting process began. "I could hardly believe the picture. Here was clearly some bone growth! I removed the cast, felt the leg, and found that the pieces were all stuck together. John watched, and when I was done, lifted his leg into the air triumphantly."

After extensive experiments along these lines, Dr. Becker concluded: "Cells exposed to positive silver ions profoundly stimulate healing in a way unlike any known natural process. Whatever its precise mode of action may be, the electrically generated silver ion can produce enough cells for blastulas; it has restored my belief that full regeneration of limbs and other body parts can be accomplished in humans."

Dr. Becker's experiments seem to show that Colloidal Silver not only kills the pathogens, but also produces dramatic healing of tissue such as the re-growth of skin on the leg, as mentioned above. The silver ion produces some cells with no differentiation. These cells can turn into any cell that is needed. Only these de-differentiated cells can be used to create the cells necessary to replace destroyed cells such as in a wound, or to rebuild missing tissue. It seems to be for this reason that Colloidal Silver heals injuries without scarring, or at least greatly reduces scarring, while greatly accelerating the reconstruction of general healing of wounds. Scar tissue develops when de-differentiated cells are in short supply. Therefore it would seem, from the evidence at hand, that CS could reduce or prevent internal scarring and promote healing after surgery.

Other Medical Uses:

In "Report: Colloidal Silver, Health Consciousness, Vol. 15, No.4", it is stated "Silver aids the developing fetus in growth, health, and eases the delivery and recovery." Hospitals routinely use it in new-born infants' eyes to prevent infection caused blindness. Silver seems to be even more promising against AIDS, and there seems to be no doubt that silver supports the T-cells. It is strongly suggested by research scientists such as Dr. Gary Smith and others that Silver ions are essential to the immune system. Marvin Robey, has personally used a strong dose of Colloidal Silver (4 Oz. Of 500 parts per million) for a cold in its early stages. It provided relief in two hours and cured the cold completely in about 24 hours. Others say that it quickly cures their colds in more advanced stages...

Physiological Information about CS:

The body's ability to process the tiny atoms of Colloidal Silver makes silver build-up in the body impossible. The Environmental Protection Agency's Poison Control Centre reports a "no toxicity" listing for CS. If particles are small enough you can even drink arsenic! Examining a bottle of colloidal minerals from a local health store you may notice nickel, arsenic and lead among the trace minerals on the ingredients list.

CS is the only form of silver that can be used safely as a supplement. It is absorbed into the tissues at a slow enough rate that is not irritating to tissues, unlike silver nitrate which reacts violently with tissues because of its caustic action.

The body has a vital need for silver to produce new healthy cells. Since our blood is also colloid, the harmonious way the colloids enter the body may well make colloidal silver the safest medicine on earth. Dr. Robert O. Becker, M.D., says that a deficiency of silver in the diet contributes to disease. In fact he found that those with low levels of silver in their body had frequent colds, flu, and sicknesses. He feels that a silver deficiency can be the cause of improper functioning of the immune system.

Used In Space Shuttle:

When will we see silver in our everyday life for non-medical use? It seems it is already more prominent in our lives than most people realize. In health consciousness, vol. 15, No. 4, Pg. 5 we read: "in the former Soviet Union, silver is used to sterilize recycled water aboard space shuttles. NASA has also selected a silver/water system for its space shuttle. Internationally, many airlines use silver water filters to guarantee passenger safety against water borne diseases such as dysentery. The Swiss government has approved use of such silver water filters in homes and offices. In the U.S. some city municipalities use silver in the treatment of sewage. Silver works so well in purifying water that it is sometimes used to purify swimming pool water. It does not sting the eyes as chlorine does, and it does kill mosquito larva. An experiment conducted in Nebraska demonstrates its effectiveness. Fifty gallons of raw sewage were pumped into a pool without any disinfectant. A standard measure of contamination is the count of E. coli, a bacteria organism found in the intestinal tract. The count soared to 7000. Coli cells per milliliter of water. When the water was exposed to silver electrodes, within three hours it was completely free of E. coli."

How You Can Use Colloidal Silver:

Add CS to drinking water when on holiday or camping. Sterilize anything from tooth brushes to surgical instruments, spray on garbage to prevent decay odors, disinfect dish cloths, cutting boards; add when canning, preserving or bottling fruits and vegetables; spray in shoes and between toes to kill fungus; disinfect bath water, use as gargle, douche, colon irrigation, nasal spray; drop onto bandages and plasters to hasten healing time; soak dentures; spray refrigerator, freezer, food storage containers to stop mildew, mold, wood rot, fungi. Use to spray pet's bedding, use in cleaning and mopping solutions. Spray on the top of open jam jars, and food lids before closing to prevent mold. Spray air ducts; use in final washing machine rinse cycle, and dishwashers. Spray around plant roots to stop rot; spray foliage to remove aphids and mold; use inside gloves and under fingernails, rinse fruit and vegetables, use in shampoos and rinsing water; spray pets and use in pet drinking water, spray carpets, wipe telephone mouth-pieces , headphones, hearing aids; spray mattresses and allow to dry to kill dust mites; clean combs and glasses. Apply to baby for diaper rash and spray inside of diapers. Clean bathrooms, kitchens, floors, underwear, pillowcases etc. etc.

Swishing the solution briefly under the tongue before swallowing ensures faster absorption and destroys mouth bacteria. In several days CS will have accumulated in the tissues sufficiently for benefits to begin. It is eliminated via the kidneys, lymph and bowel within 3 weeks.

CS is painless on cuts and abrasions, in open wounds, in the nostrils for sinus stuffy nose and even in babies eyes, because unlike antiseptics it dies not destroy tissue cells. Inside the body silver forms no toxic features. It cannot react or interfere with any other medication being taken.

Dr. Hulda Clark feels that sufficient CS is ingested from cleaning the teeth. Perhaps more is needed in certain conditions. Other doctors suggest one or two teaspoons daily.

There is no limit for external use. In general, modern Colloidal Silver is of much better quality than it was in the 1930's and 40's due to modern knowledge of how to produce it. Still better news is that you can produce colloidal silver of the finest quality yourself for pennies a bottle. This way, you know it is fresh and you have a better idea of the concentration and quality.

When current is applied to silver in solution the particles that break off will always be the same size: 1.26 angstroms (.000126 microns). This is so small that its nearest rival is an atom. Very simple, inexpensive, easily used and maintainable equipment is now available by several manufacturers to make your own Colloidal Silver of the finest quality, absolutely fresh. To purchase ready-made CS is highly expensive. To make it for yourself via a little machine costs only cents. Important: Dr. Clark's comments regarding CS: "The purity of the silver is an important issue. The manufacturer of the silver should divulge this. Use only 99.99% pure silver.   (End of Quoting.)

As an important follow-up, here is a listing of medical applications for Colloidal Silver which has been compiled from several medical sources, and included with the material copied. I have now reprinted the list in a more directly alphabetical order. You should now be able to check out any condition or malady more quickly and easily.

Medical applications of colloidal silver - (This is a limited list of medical uses):

Acne, **AIDS**, Allergies, Appendicitis, Arthritis, Athlete's Foot

Bacteria, (all forms) Bladder Infection, Bleeding Gums, Blepharitis, Blood Parasites, Blood Poisoning, Boils, **Bubonic Plague**, Burns

Cancer, **Candida** (yeast infection), Canine Provirus, Canker Sores, Chilblains, Cholera, Chronic Fatigue, **Colds**, Colitis, Conjunctivitis, Cystitis

Dandruff, Dermatitis, Diabetes, **Diphtheria**, Dysentery

Ear infections, **Ebola**, Eczema, Encephalitis -- Fibrosis's, **Flu**, Furunculous

Gastritis, Gingivitis, **Gonorrhoea** -- Halitosis, Hay Fever, Haemorrhoids, Hepatitis, **Herpes** Impetigo, Indigestion -- Keratinise

Lyme disease, Lymphagitis, **Leprosy**, Leukemia - **Malaria**, Meningitis, Moles

Neurasthenia -- **Parasitic infections**, Pavo virus, Plant viruses & **fungi**, Pleurisy, **Pneumonia** (viral, fungal & bacterial), Prostate, Prurititis,   **Psoriasis**, Purulent ophthalmia, Pyorrhea

Quinsy -- Rheumatism, Rhinitis, Ringworm, Resaca

SARS, Scabies, Septic conditions (of eye, ear, nose & throat), Septicaemia, **Shingles**, Skin Cancer, Skin rashes, sore throat, **Staph infections**, Stomach flu, Stomach ulcer, Strep infection, **Syphilis**, **Scarlet fever**, Scarletina, Ciboria

Thrush (yeast infection), Thyroid, **Tonsillitis**, Tooth decay (neutralize), **Toxaemia**, Trachoma, Trench foot, **Tuberculosis**

Ulcerated stomach (ulcers) -- **Venereal diseases**, Virus (all forms)

Warts, **West Nile Virus**, **Whooping Cough** -- Yeast infection

Helpful suggestions by Patrick H. Bellringer of fourwinds10.com :

A.)   <u>Do Your Own CS With Your Own CS Generator.</u>
"You can make your own colloidal silver with a CS generator far more cheaply than purchasing CS from a health store at $10 per ounce of solution. CS generators for home use are made by various companies listed on the internet. I purchased the CS generator that I use from <u>http://www.robeysilver.com</u>. I recommend the home generator deluxe model at a cost of $180. (2007), because it has an automatic shut off control and a parts per million (ppm) control dial."

"The automatic shut-off control allows one to use a larger glass container such as a quart or two quart jar to make larger amounts of colloidal silver. The machine will shut off when the solution reaches the ppm set on the ppm control dial., usually in about one hour. One word of caution is that colloidal solutions, using electrolysis must be made using only distilled water. Any other water contains minerals which will render the passing of an electric current through it ineffective for making a proper colloidal solution."

B.)   <u>How Many (PPM's) Do You Need, For Effective Anti-Bacterial Action?</u>
"The human body utilizes colloidal silver at the rate of three to five ppm. Higher concentrations of silver are not harmful in any way, but they do not kill internal microbes more effectively. For a topical application of CS, a silver concentration of 60ppm or higher is needed. At this level, CS is also effective as an after-shave deodorant, mouth wash, for gargling and for burns, cuts, insect bites and other skin irritations.

C.)   <u>Earlier Uses of Silver in the U.S.</u>
"On a side note the early pioneers in the U.S. "old west" would put a silver dollar into a bucket of fresh milk and keep it from spoiling without refrigeration for two to three days. They also used true silverware and silver dishes which aided their

health, also, for many centuries the royal families of the world have been called "blue bloods" because of the high silver content in their blood. They stored their food in silver dishes, ate from silver plates and cups, and used true silverware. They had no modern medicine and medical doctors but remained healthy. The "commoners" could not afford silver utensils and were usually sick.

For many years my family and I have used colloidal silver with great success. We recommend one-fourth to one-half cup of colloidal silver a day as a maintenance program, if you are able to make your own CS. CS can be put into your drinking water and used throughout the day or taken at meal times to keep your body constantly supplied. Over time light will reduce the positive charge on the silver ion, causing it to precipitate from suspension.

The silver will then adhere to the walls of the container and render it unusable. This problem is corrected by storing CS in amber colored glass bottles. This gives it an indefinite shelf life. Colloidal Gold (CG) is nearly unavailable in U.S. health stores today, as are CG generators on the internet. The price of gold makes buying CG very expensive.

The U.S. government has effectively prohibited the manufacturing of CG generators, but one source is found at http://www.biophysica.com Colloidal titanium and colloidal titanium generators are nearly impossible to find in the marketplace.

The big lie is that all healing can only happen through medicines, drugs, medical techniques and expertise of the medical community. Medical doctors are honored as the Gods of healing and are paid accordingly. Behind the scenes the pharmaceutical companies control all. They fund the medical research grants at the universities to control the results, and they bribe the medical doctors to utilize their drugs and techniques by allowing the doctors to become stockholders in their pharmaceutical companies. This is all done at the expense of those who suffer from illness, and many, who are ill, have become so from the medications and techniques of the medical community.

Colloidal silver is kept secret by the pharmaceutical industry for two very important reasons. The first reason, of course, is that the effectiveness and availability of CS would severely cut into the profits the drug companies make today on all the various antibiotics, flu and cold remedies. The second reason is that CS cannot be patented. The Food and Drug Administration has classified CS as a pre 1938 drug, which makes it exempt from current patent laws. If a product cannot be patented and a monopoly held on it in the marketplace, it cannot demand a high price. Therefore CS is worthless to the pharmaceutical profiteers. In fact they are fearful that colloidal silver may return to public use and have worked hard to keep it hidden.

Is it any wonder that colloidal silver which can stop viruses such as West Nile, AIDS, Ebola, Bubonic Plague, and SARS, is kept hidden from public use? Something so inexpensive, so easy to make, and so accessible to the public as colloidal silver would cause so much good health as to wipe out whole sections of the pharmaceuticals in thousands of hospitals and drug stores. Such is the trillion dollar drug lie. Can you imagine a world without harmful molds and bacteria? Can you imagine a world without the common cold, without AIDS, without the "flu", without venereal disease, without SARS? That is the world of colloidal silver. **We certainly are people of the lie!** " (end quoting.)

Further Comments Concerning - Medicine?

If any medical doctor dares to say that he can cure or has cured anything, he could be banned from the medical association. I am totally aware of that situation, as a close and dear friend of mine, Dr. Carl Reich, wrote the book, "The Calcium Factor" along with Bob Barefoot, another friend of mine who is an organic chemist, and who has also since written a book called "Death by Diet".

Dr. Reich was ejected from the medical association in Alberta for eliminating debilitating conditions in senior citizens by providing them with mega doses of vitamins and minerals. The end result was that their medical care was costing them about $40.00 per year through Alberta Health Care, plus cheaper vitamins and minerals rather than the usual $120.00 per year plus expensive prescriptions. That angered the medical association, as Alberta Health Care was blindly funding their set up system of things, and they had Carl disbarred. What else is new at the present time in this marvelous world?

The pharmaceutical companies, which are the most profitable companies in this world, control our medical schools etc., and indoctrinate our medical and nursing students. That has been a fact of life since the Rockefeller business empire bought into the drug and pharmaceutical industry. Did you know that the average difference between cost of production and retail price in the pharmaceutical business is a bit more than 30 to 1..?

Heart Disease is another situation where suppression of information is the rule. Anything made from natural products, or the use of particular herbals and even some ordinary things to lower the symptoms of or even to ultimately cure a "heart condition" have been suppressed to the fullest extent possible for a long time. Heart disease is an extremely large and profitable business for the medical "profession". The pharmaceutical companies give all of our "doctors" a kickback on every prescription they write for chemical junk, and they never see a dime for far more effective herbals etc.

A few years ago, my wife and I dealt with a person who was then 71 years old, and had in the previous year suffered a massive heart attack, when he was visiting in the state of Washington, and attending a local fair.

He was taken to Seattle by helicopter, and given emergency

medical attention. When he had stabilized, he was advised that he should return to Calgary, and arrange at the first opportunity to get himself scheduled for triple bypass surgery to deal with the problem. He returned to Calgary, arranged for his bypass surgery, which was scheduled for 4 months later, and contemplated his situation.

He bought a book which suggested that Cayenne Pepper in continuous large doses might clean out or eliminate most of the plaque buildup in his arteries and circulatory system. He bought a large supply, and began taking triple zero capsules two or three times a day. He began noticing some improvement in his general condition after taking the capsules for the first month, so he continued taking them regularly.

When he was close to his scheduled time for the recommended operation, he went to his doctor for a checkup, and he no longer had any symptoms or evidence of any blockages in his circulatory system. In other words, he was in virtually perfect health for a person of his age, and there was no longer any reason for having the operation.

Ref: "Left For Dead" By R.F. Quinn

Chapter 3

E X T R A T E R R E S T R E A L S

There continues to be a very intense world wide effort to deny their existence, and suppress all contact and any other information related to our ET brothers. - since 1954
. . . Numerous extraterrestrial craft have crashed in the U.S., and were recovered. The first one was recovered in 1941, followed by a quiet period until 1947...

The first one we heard of through our very restricted media was the one that was brought down by radar at Roswell New Mexico, and its existence was carefully and forcibly suppressed, almost immediately. At the time, Coronet Magazine published an issue covering the story of the crashed discoid craft, and the recovery of a number of aliens, said to include 3 dead ones and one still alive.

That entire edition of Coronet Magazine was confiscated and destroyed. Another disc was recovered in the Socorro area of New Mexico, and a third, a short distance into Mexico. All 3 of the recovered craft ended up in secret storage at hangar 18, Wright-Patterson AFB, Dayton Ohio. Virgil Armstrong had been an Air Force security officer at the site, and told me the truth of the matter, in 1982.

Before the cover up situation had begun, in 1947, a pilot by the name of Matthew Arnold had encountered a group of U.F.O.'s flying in formation close to the mountains in eastern Washington State. Pictures were taken of that group of flying discs, and were published in a couple of newspapers.

Our lying and devious secret leadership, behind and above the level of our top elected officials did not want us to become aware that we are not alone in this galaxy, and that there are other highly sentient races out there from our neighboring solar systems. It is a fact that almost every star you can see in the sky out there is a sun, much like ours in many cases, and almost every one of them is a complete solar system, usually with 6 to 12 planets. Other races out there, including many who look much like us, are thousands and even millions of years beyond us in terms of technology. Most of those races are far more intelligent than we are, as they have had a much longer time to evolve.

At the present time, the fact that all of the extraterrestrial human and other sentient races out there are peaceful, and have no subjective or controlling interest in dominating us, is being kept very secret by our controllers. - They have set up an emotional control grid to keep us in ignorance and bondage, and if you don't think so, you haven't taken a very close look.

Ref: The Day After Roswell - by Col. Corso (U.S. Army - Ret.)

Those ET folks could come to visit us and show us how to set up and run an entirely peaceful society, like a true republic, like theirs, in which each and every individual citizen is sovereign, and all energy sources are free energy devices. Also, their governments must perform according to their wishes, or be run off and replaced, as the common citizens may choose.

If we were to think that our marvelous controllers were not the most powerful and capable people, we might lose confidence in their ability to manage and control us. There has been severe suppression of information concerning contact with the Sirians and the Pleiadeans and those from Andromeda, Hercules, Altair, Pegasus and Centaurus, who all look quite similar to us. They all have technology which is thousands of years beyond the best of ours. This includes space travel at the speed of thought, which is many times the speed of light. Even our reptilian neighbors out there, from Orion can travel 80+ light years in about 7 minutes. How's that for an eye opener, compared to the elementary bullshit you are being fed by NASA and other "official" sources..??

The Pleiadeans in particular, have been telling our secret government since about 1947, that they should not be making, testing and deploying nuclear weapons. They have also been seriously warning us about rampant atmospheric pollution in particular, from hydrocarbon fuels and fallout from nuclear explosions and accidents at nuclear power plants. It is interesting to note two things. Our sun is in the Pleiades star group in the constellation of Taurus, and secondly, the closest human occupied planet is only 4.39 light years away from us, in the constellation of Centaurus.

This galaxy has a central sun, and all of the constellations of thousands of stars each, are in orbit around the central sun, and their total period of rotation is about 206 million years. Our sun with its solar system is the 8th. star in the Pleiadean star group in the constellation of Taurus, according to our astronomers. However, our galactic neighbors are telling us that there are more like 2000+ stars or solar systems in the Pleiadean star group. They are telling us that when we start exploring the galaxy, that is one of the surprising things we will be able to confirm for ourselves.

As far as our sun is concerned, it is in orbit around a major star of our Pleiadean star group, called Alcyone, and our own astronomers are aware that our sun orbits around Alcyone one time each 25,000 to 26,000 years. There is an exact published figure, but I don't remember it at the moment. I am just giving you an idea how large these systems are, and how infinitely small each of us little humans is in the scheme of things. What I see there, is that a central sun, a very major star at the center of each constellation has a large secondary group of stars rotating around it, and each of those secondary stars has a small number of smaller stars, which rotate around each of them. Each of those at a third stage level is a separate solar system. In our particular case, our sun is one of 8 of the more clearly visible stars rotating around one of those larger secondary stars as mentioned above.

Every constellation appears to have its central star, just like our Taurus constellation does, and the total range outward from the central star in each case to the farthest away solar system rotating around it is greater than 200 light years in most cases. Everything in this universe goes from macro to micro, from stars and planets down to molecules and atoms. The deeper you look, the more you see. It all fits together...

I cordially invite you to disagree with what I am saying. However, I then place upon you the intellectual and moral responsibility of proving me wrong. In the case of you proving me wrong, if that indeed, becomes obvious, I will be most pleased to have that confirmed. The corrected information would be put into my next book in this series. Also, you would be acknowledged for your clarification (s).

We, as cute little humans, are rather insignificant in the scale of things, in spite of our assumed levels of higher intelligence. We are analogous to sub atomic particles buzzing around on one of the atoms of a particular molecule. Also, biological life in its myriad of forms is likely to exist in all of those other solar systems. It is also very likely that a serious percentage of those solar systems are somewhat similar to our own, as you will begin to observe in chapter 6.

Our secret leaders and hidebound establishments don't want the rest of us to even think in those terms, as such truths make them all look rather unimportant. As far as our secret leaders are concerned, they have not been telling us so far that there is really a breathable atmosphere on both the moon and mars, albeit in each case, rather thin, and that there are plants growing on the moon.

To get on with the government intrigue related to those things in the U.S.A., all of the following information is being quoted directly from a book of The Phoenix Journals, dictated by Commander Gyorgos Ceres Hatonn, of the Pleiadean Star Fleet.

The book is called "**SPACE GATE**" - "**THE VEIL REMOVED**". The Phoenix Journals are available for reading, downloading and printing on the **fourwinds10.com** website, anytime you want to obtain a lot of accurate and truthful information, not available from our standard controlled and suppressed media sources.

"President Eisenhower, by secret memorandum, NSC 5401/1 established a permanent committee to be known as Majority 12 (MJ-12) to oversee and conduct all activities concerned with the alien question. This organization was supposedly created to explain the purpose of questionable activities and Clandestine "above top secret" meetings where speculative contents were being leaked to the congress and the press. MJ-12 was originally made up of: (1.) Nelson Rockefeller, then (2.) Director of Central Intelligence, Allen Welsh Dulles. (3.) Secretary of State, John Foster Dulles. (4.) Secretary of Defense, Charles E. Wilson. (5.) Chairman of the Joint Chiefs of Staff, Admiral Arthur W. Radford, (6.) Director of the Federal Bureau of Investigation, J. Edgar Hoover, and six men from the Executive Committee of the Council on Foreign Relations known as the "wise men". It was claimed these men were all members of a secret society of scholars that called themselves "The Jason Society", whose members in turn supposedly came from the prestigious (secret) societies of Harvard and Yale, the "Scroll and Key" and the "Skull and Bones".

This group was made up over the years of the top officers and directors of the Council on Foreign Relations and later the Trilateral Commission. George Bush Sr., Gordon Dean and Zbignew Berzezinski were prominent among them. The most important and influential of the "wise men" who served on MJ-12 were John McCloy, Robert Lovett, Avril Harriman, Charles Bohlen, George Kennan and Dean Acheson. Their policies lasted well into the decade of the 1970's. President Eisenhower, as well as the first 6 members of MJ-12 were from the government and were also members of the Council on Foreign Relations.

In November of 1955, NSC-5412/2 was issued establishing a study committee to explore "All factors which are involved in the making and implementing of foreign policy in the nuclear age" as a neatly laid out plan to camouflage the real point of the matter, (the "alien" question and problem).

By secret executive memorandum NSC 5411 in 1954, President Eisenhower had commissioned the study group to "examine all the facts, evidence, lies, and deceptions and discover the truth of the "alien question". NSC 5412/2 (mentioned above) was a cover which was necessary when the press began inquiring as to the purpose of regular meetings of such important persons. These meetings were first dubbed the "Quantico" meetings which began in 1954, and were held at Quantico Marine Base.

I could continue on with more comments etc. concerning the further evolution of the three main world governing bodies which continue to be tied directly back to MJ-12, and remain responsible for maintaining total secrecy concerning extraterrestrials. A couple of important agencies must be mentioned, because they are very critical and deeply involved in "secret government operations" and "black projects".

Firstly, this world has been, and presently continues to be controlled by the Bilderbergers, The Council on Foreign Relations, The Trilateral Commission, and then on down to Presidents, Prime Ministers and other "elected"? politicians. In the deeper background of things, the Jesuits and the "Black Pope" of the Jesuits, are quietly at the top end of the Illuminati. The Bilderbergers, particularly the key banking family factions thereof, along with most senior members of "Skull & Bones" and "Scroll & Key", and 32nd level and upward at the top end of the Freemasons, are very likely to be members of the Illuminati. The Illuminati are completely Luciferians, and the Freemasons start out at that level.

The two most important agencies involved directly in all of the secret government's black operations are **N.S.A**. (The National Security Agency), which is now at the top, and the **CIA** (Central Intelligence Agency). The **NSA** is the agency secretly in control of all of the black budgets concerning building and deployment of secret anti-gravity inter-stellar space craft, which the secret government has been flying around since the 1960's, for example. The **CIA** is in total control of the world illicit drug trade, and the horrendous profits from that system of things is funneled into the black budgets of the **NSA**. The **CIA** is the organization which carries out a high percentage of assassinations of inventors and scientists who come up with new technology to replace or eliminate the large scale monopoly energy operations out there, such as the oil cartels, and the electrical utility cartels. Their top management are tied back to the secret government group, who control and direct the **CIA** etc...

One other thing of great importance, particularly as you observe current things going on, is the so-called **"Zionists"** who appear to be the war-mongering faction of the present U.S. government, as they were continuing to movie toward total and complete dictatorship, in 2007.

For a more complete background on the clear motivation of the **Zionists**, going back to long before the French Revolution, please access & read if you can, **"the 24 Zionist Protocols"**, as mentioned in Chapter 21. Those had to be left out of this book, as they are quite elaborate, and would come to 65+ pages. They do relate to every war and economic depression, withheld information, political payoffs, assassinations, etc. The **Zionists** also created, and presently own and control **the communist system,** and any government under that banner, **and also** absolutely **dominate** our so-called **"capitalist"** governments.

Continuous Suppression & Various Happenings In The Meantime

Let's go back to the early days, when the CIA was a brand new operation, in 1949. Back in those days, James Forrestal, your then Secretary of Defense in the U.S.A., began to object to all the secrecy.

(Murder #1)

When he began to argue and talk to leaders of the opposition party and leaders of the Congress about the alien problem, he was promptly asked to resign his appointment. Secret government? Absolutely the case, even in the old days, back in 1949. He expressed his fears to a lot of people, and rightly believed that he was under surveillance. Most of his peers in the Congress were totally ignorant of the alien situation, due to near total suppression then already in place. His fellow members of congress at that time, simply began to assume that Forrestal was paranoid and schizophrenic.

In any event, the authorities took care of Mr. Forrestal, declaring that he had a mental breakdown, and they placed him in the Bethesda Naval Hospital. It was made sure of, that Forrestal was placed in isolation, so he could not tell any secrets concerning U.F.O. information, etc. In the early hours of May 22, 1949, agents of the CIA tied a sheet around his neck, fastened the other end to a fixture in his room, and pushed him out the window. The sheet tore, and he plummeted to his death. Other "suicides" were arranged and carried out since that point in time, as convenient means to eliminate individuals who intended to "spill the beans" in spite of the tight cover set up by MJ-12..

(More murders quietly arranged)

By 1953, at least ten additional discs had been recovered since the Roswell incident. There were 25 to 30 dead aliens, and four live ones. The figures are probably larger than that, as these statistics were taken from government information which was deliberately falsified. Most of those crashes of discoid anti-gravity craft were "shoot downs", because such craft were very vulnerable to interfering energy fields, particularly RADAR, and when those craft are manifested in visible format (uncloaked) they are vulnerable. Back in that time frame, only the U.S. was shooting down aliens. Although it is a very distasteful thing to say, **most live alien survivors were put to death rather quickly on orders of MJ-12**. - They were, and are, uncaring, cold-blooded murdering criminals.

That is a truly horrendous situation, as there was not a single aggressive or less than peaceful alien among all of those executed by the marvelous U.S. government, and its secret agencies. That begs the question once again, Who runs the U.S. government, and gives them the right to carry out random or large scale murder whenever it has been convenient for the illuminati, wanting everything kept secret. -- **Murder is not justifiable anywhere in God's world.**

Eisenhower's Meetings with Extraterrestrials and the U.S. / Alien Treaty:

In 1954, then president, Dwight D. Eisenhower met at Holloman Air Force Base with a race of Extraterrestrials described as "large nosed grey aliens". In that meeting, a basic agreement was reached, leading to a second meeting, where a secret "treaty" was signed. - Maybe those "bleached" little guys were earlier forerunners of the Khazarians. (many of them also have large noses).

Although it is not mentioned in my referred material, I have read the background In other earlier publications concerning those two secret meetings in particular. The date of the second meeting I am about to refer to was October 20th. 1954... This follow-up meeting was held at Edwards Air Force Base. Along with Eisenhower, the meeting was attended by Bernard Baruch, and the Roman Catholic Archbishop of Los Angeles, James Francis McIntyre. An earlier publication identified one other personage of some high position in the U.S., who had attended that meeting.

As to the meetings and the "Treaty" agreed upon by the secret government of the U.S., with a race of aliens, the most important consideration relating to those activities is that as early as 1954, U.S. citizens were kept totally unaware of such things.. **Your totally subjective leaders decided that each and all of you as citizens of the U.S. were not entitled to such information**, and were likely to go into a state of total confusion, leading to anarchy. You were looked upon as "sheep" or "lemmings" by your secret government leaders, and it was surely felt then, and still is by them, that you would react and behave like dumb animals. Those folks look upon themselves as the "elites" as far as the rest of us human folks are concerned. Attitudes of that kind have been common to certain wealthy and controlling families in Europe, England and then the U.S., for centuries, and long before that, in Israel, and following through to Rome etc.

The prevailing attitude of the U.S. secret government becomes even more reprehensible when terms and conditions of the "treaty" are considered. The "Greys" stated that they were from a planet in the solar system of a red star in the Constellation of Orion, which we have labelled as "Betelgeuse". They are taller than the Zetas, who are noted for their large heads, with large flat eyes, and a comparatively flat nose. The "Zetas" are from the Zeta Reticuli solar system. The greys have a far more prominent nose, and tend to be negative and dominating, while the Zetas try to be peaceful and benevolent.

Purported contents of the "Treaty" were as follows:
1. The aliens were not allowed to interfere in the affairs of the secret government. (Nothing was really conceded there, as under the rules of the Intergalactic council, they would not be allowed to interfere in any case...) - And further to that the secret government agreed not to interfere with the aliens.
2. The Greys would provide advanced technology, and would assist with technological development.

3. The Greys would not make a treaty with any other earth nation.

4. The Greys could abduct humans on a limited and periodic basis for the purpose of medical examination and monitoring of our development. The humans involved would not be harmed, and would be returned to the point of abduction, and have no memory of the event. The aliens would furnish the secret government (MJ-12), with a list of all human contacts and abductees on a regularly scheduled basis.

5. It was agreed that each nation would receive the Ambassador from the other, as long as the agreement remained in force.

6. The Greys and the U.S. would exchange 16 personnel with each other, with the Americans going to Orion, and the Greys coming to the U.S. This exchange would occur with the change of personnel on a regularly scheduled basis.

7. It was agreed that bases would be constructed underground for the use of the Greys, and that two underground bases would be constructed for the joint use of the Greys and the U.S. secret government.

What Happened Next?

Underground bases were built beneath Indian Reservations, beginning in the 4 corners area, where Colorado, New Mexico, Arizona and Utah come together, then at S-4, seven miles south of the western border of Area 51, and this one would become known as "Dreamland". Its original code name was "The Far Side of The Moon", which was quite appropriate, considering the experimental work **done at S-4, including test fying saucer" craft, beginning in 1957** (Project Redlight), as earlier provided by the Greys. Ironically, **the U.S. and Russia both had discoid craft parked at a secret base on the moon, by the time the first American astronauts landed on the moon**. (They saw those craft, and were sworn to secrecy under threat of death.)

(With regard to the Indian Reservations, does anybody believe the Native Americans were contacted before any of the bases were built under their reservations? I suspect that did not happen.)

There is also a huge installation in New Mexico. (All Alien areas were put under the complete control of the U.S. Navy, obviously for the purpose of side tracking and obscuring any effort to look into the situation, as to technology or funding.)

The White House underground **SECRET** construction fund was set up by President Eisenhower in 1957. This fund was used to build more than 75 deep underground facilities. These included the Alien bases either directly for, or for use along with the Greys, plus many more which were classified as "DUMB" bases, (Deep Underground Military Bases).

To bring you more completely up to date, as of this writing, by **1995-96, Phil Schneider, a geologist for the U.S. Government** (the secret side) **reported that a total of 131 underground installations** had been completed. **Serge Monast,** another separate source, being an **investigative reporter from Quebec in Canada, wrote two books on the subject before being assassinated.**

He covered about 129 of those underground establishments which had been privately revealed to him by disenchanted Americans who know they were being used for criminal purposes by the secret government. (This only covers the U.S., and there are many hundreds more of underground installations around the world, from Canada to Russia, China, Britain etc. etc. - (We are talking about a secret world government, not just in the U.S.)

The types of underground facilities referred to in the U.S. include the following:

1) The first in series were those intended for the U.S. Government, cabinet and senior officials, and their families and entourage etc.

2) The original small series of large facilities to accommodate

the Greys, and those which were for joint use of the Greys and U.S. Government appointed personnel, including Scientists & Engineers etc.

3) Small city or large town types for the One World Order "Elite" folks, their families and large numbers of workers and maintenance personnel.

4) Very large underground establishments referred to as "DUMB", which was an abbreviation for "deep underground military bases". Remember the big bang in Oklahoma City? - Murrah Building? (That was a tiny nuclear bomb warm-up for 9-11, which was to come later.) - One of the "DUMB" bases was said to have been accessible from the Murrah building.

5) Very large and elaborately equipped underground detention facilities, with some of them including the modern equivalent of gas chambers and super crematoriums. I have also read where two boatloads of guillotines were delivered to the U.S., which were provided for such underground facilities.

6) Underground manufacturing plants being used by various builders of U.S. based and highly secret anti-gravity equipped and driven aircraft and space craft.

7) Secret underground mining facilities, for Uranium in particular, one of which is located beneath an Indian reservation in the U.S., according to a totally reliable source I have been accessing.

Aside from the above mentioned types of underground facilities, I am aware through the many sources I have searched out over the past 35+ years, that there is a very complete high speed underground rapid transit system in existence beneath the U.S. Gleaned information indicates that the transit system connects all of the 131 or more underground establishments of all kinds mentioned above.

Further to that, another legitimate source suggests complete routes back and forth from Washington D.C. to the west coast of the U.S., probably ending up at a surface military base somewhere between San Francisco and Los Angeles. Information from a third, much earlier source, and seemingly unrelated, reveals that some of the deep under-ground rapid transit system tunnels were in place thousands of years before America was "discovered'. (The "Tao" civilization - as described by Edgar Cayce.)

Here is one of the last items I will cover before moving from underground to above ground. Although it was more than 35 years ago, there was a confrontation between the Greys and U.S. representatives in one of their jointly operated underground "laboratory" bases. It has been reported in at least three sources I have checked out, that there was a confrontation, started by the U.S. side, against the Greys in one of the underground establishments. At that time, it was reported that about 60 U.S. personnel were killed through use of hand-held beam weapons by the Greys. A retreat by the U.S. contingent followed immediately, and there was no further action between the U.S. and the Greys for some time, until a truce and continued cooperation agreement was reached, a couple of years later. As a point of interest, Phil Schneider, the U.S. government geologist mentioned previously, had been wounded by the Greys in that skirmish, and had survived.

You may have had your small world experiences like I have. Here is a very interesting one that I had, back in the summer of 1981. I happened to be staying at a quaint and interesting older Motel, situated not far from the public library in Phoenix Arizona, and was at that time setting up an extractive metallurgy project at Gilbert, Arizona, not far out of Phoenix. The bar and lounge area was unoccupied, early one evening, except for a bearded fellow who greeted me with a smile, and asked if I would like to join him at the bar. I was pleased to have some company, so he and I quickly introduced our-selves, and began to discuss a number of interesting things.

Soon, this gentleman, whose name was Virgil Armstrong, asked me if I had any interest in Unidentified Flying Objects, then more commonly referred to as Flying Saucers. I told him that I was quite familiar with the subject, having read everything I could find on the subject since about 1963.

He said that he was pleased to hear that, and he had an interesting story to tell, concerning the Roswell incident, where he had been involved at the crash site, as a member of an Air Force intelligence unit. Almost everything he revealed to me at that time, verbally, and further by means of a couple of cassette tapes he gave me to take home and review, has since been completely corroborated by two or three other sources. However, one thing in particular stuck in my mind that was not directly corroborated by the later sources. The sheet metal outside body surface of the craft was hard to dent with a 14 pound sledge hammer, even though it was not much thicker than ordinary letter quality paper.

He had also mentioned a live alien being captured, and that a couple of others were dead at the time the craft was recovered. The recovered craft was slowly and carefully moved at night, by truck, in small increments over a period of time, finally ending up at Wright Patterson Air Force Base at Dayton Ohio.

Now is the time to mention the small alien humanoid, who was somewhere between a Zeta Reticulan and a Grey in height, and hairless like they are, but having different eyes, and nose from those two. Also, it was learned a few days later, after this marvelous little fellow was checked out more carefully, that his blood system was chlorophyll, the same as plants. His assimilation and elimination systems were also virtually the same as with plants.

For whatever reasons, probably including malnutrition, the highly intelligent little fellow died about a year and a half after his craft hit the ground in the Roswell area. It was said by another source, that the little fellow was from a planet with a higher content of carbon dioxide in its atmosphere, which is ideal for plants. Those humanoids had evolved to full consciousness, developed space craft, and were now exploring the galaxy, like many others more and less similar to us. Our atmosphere has a higher oxygen content, and is likely to be similar to many other solar systems in this galaxy. The high carbon dioxide atmosphere is more unusual.

Since I am trying to be in the teaching business rather than providing a bunch of scattered items of interest, or entertainment, we will now look into who is there and what has been going on in this region of our Milky Way Galaxy. As we proceed next with Chapter 4, a few preliminaries will be provided, and we will get into the matter of our Galactic Neighbors.

Other References: Behold a Pale Horse - by William C. Cooper - Phoenix Journals archives - check on the net - http://www.fourwinds10.com & Particularly, drboylan.com Dr. Boylan covered the 1964 meeting between the extraterrestrials and MJ-12, and our Earth-based criminals made their positions and ours as common citizens clear at that time.

Chapter 4

MEDIA, WITHELD INFORMATION-DEFINED LIMITATIONS (LIES) + WELL ORGANIZED & CAREFULLY PLANNED SUPPRESSION

Each time I reach out and start explaining supposedly "new things", the starting point often does not include the usually taught or accepted criteria or standards which might assure us that what is being said has any "officially approved" meaning, let alone "acceptance". So much for the B.S. department, now let's get on with the real truth, and play catch up toward a world of truth and perhaps also eventually, toward individual sovereignty and freedom.

In any event, there have been a number of sources of psychically dictated information from various extraterrestrial sources over the last 45 years, from the Pleiadeans, Sirians, Arcturians and a few others. Those of you out there who are busy protecting your own ignorance (based on mind control applied by your totally controlled media, and your churches as well) have been led to accept that so-called psychic sources are "not to be believed".

Funny those things should be that way, when so many things in the bible, including the book of revelation were obviously psychically dictated information. Sounds like the hypocrites are at it again! A serious percentage of psychic sources are far more reliable than any of our present controlled media. Quite often they are our only source of the real truth about anything the controlled media is seriously trying to hide. They tell us who is lying, and why. Media news is 100% edited, & psychic sources are not edited. Folks on the other side just do not lie, as they have nothing to gain, and no reason to lie.

Our controlled media can effectively and broadly influence and control most other forms of communication, to maintain edicts and lies as we are led down the garden path. However, the only sources they really cannot control in a broader sense, as they now do with regular media, are either psychic, or provided by our galactic friends by means of mind frequency communication.

Since the subject of mind frequency has now been mentioned, and you won't see it again in this book until T. Galen Hyeronemous is mentioned, I want you to knock down your presently imposed and accepted barriers and limitations in that area. The dark side secret government in the U.S. in particular, has had the ability to directly influence the human mind, plant thoughts therein, and dictate to humans like zombies, and that technology has been in use since the 1970's. The only difference between this situation and that of the Sirian's and Pleiadean civilizations, is that they are a couple of million years ahead, and can access you directly, if they want to, by tuning in your own totally unique mind frequency, eliminating any other coercion or steps, and they are not stupid enough to lie.

The Sirians and Pleiadeans, along with our ascended masters (5th. Dimension), have been providing a high percentage of the information as published in the Phoenix Journals, the earlier CONTACT newspaper, and further to some extent more recently on http://www.fourwinds10.com. Such information would never have been revealed or published in any segment of the regular controlled media.

Please also keep this information in mind when you are reading the descriptions of 22 ET civilizations, as originally dictated to Sheldan Nidle. **He has given me permission to include those descriptions in this book.** Sheldan was given an implant by the Sirians as a child, and has had all of the information dictated to him by that means.

It must be borne in mind that the internet is also the main source of genuine and truthful news for those of us who are familiar with it, know where to look, and the quality of our sources. That is why the present governments in the U.S., England and China have been trying to legislate the internet out of business.

The same world controllers, who are denying all of this stuff, are now planning on using implants on as many of us as possible to control us more completely. Sounds a bit odd, doesn't it? They have taken the "hypocritical oath", agreeing to lie as necessary to maintain the "party line". (Freemasons & Illuminati?)

This situation is analogous to that of the medical profession where their Hypocratic Oath became a hypocritical oath ($$$), a long time ago.

Psychic sources have been here throughout all of history, and at the present time, are usually far more accurate and truthful than anything you are likely to see in our totally controlled and politically correct newspapers, or in our totally controlled and directed radio and TV sources.

One of the bothersome problems most mind-controlled folks out there have to face is that a series of our most recognized institutions have also been lying to us. This includes our marvelous churches, who are only dealing with a totally controlled and carefully suppressed system of spiritual information. The Vatican and a number of our secret societies are remarkably similar in the way they operate, and the way they control, suppress and completely hide information.

Reincarnation is an absolute fact, and the only way we progress spiritually back to our source is by learning incrementally over a very long period of time.

Our longer term memory, over a series of many lifetimes is a soul record. Our memory within this lifetime is contained within the cells of our bodies. We are taught and told otherwise because our current system of control, including our governments, wants to keep us ignorant, subservient, pliable and controllable, **or they would be** out on their asses in short order…

What your church has been teaching you is only what puts them in control, and keeps them there. Don't be fooled by their piousness. Their system(s), like the other things specified in our controlled media, which are supposedly most important in your life, are based on control. It is "nice" to be prim and proper, and not a problem to any part of the "establishment", but you really should be a sovereign citizen, and not a "lemming", or do you have a problem with that?

My position in these matters has been that I would sooner be a bothersome person for the establishment than to be some kind of a Zombie paying allegiance to a group of self-appointed egotistical fools. Those folks have labeled themselves as the "elite" of this world, and think they should lead and manipulate us. Their most powerful primary means of control include the world's money system, a serious majority of our hydrocarbon energy companies and related refineries, virtually all of the major media, worldwide, and very tight inside control of our largest religious institutions, newspapers and other public media.

At the present time, we would be labeled as "terrorists", by "homeland security" in the U.S. As the plan for enslavement has progressed to 2007, anyone disagreeing with the European Union is now to be labeled as a "terrorist", under their most recent statutes. What else is new, as our "elite" controllers keep pushing their "One World Order"? - - -
Check out the EU. It is run by un-elected appointees, as a total dictatorship. The banking families controlling this world started out in Europe. Do you think they would settle for less than that ???

HERE IS ANOTHER SITUATION WHERE VERY IMPORTANT TECHNOLOGY WAS TOTALLY SUPPRESSED AWAY BACK IN THE 1940'S.

This relates to psychic frequencies and being able to communicate that way, without wires or other connections of any kind, or related time or distance

limitations. Apparently the speed of thought leaves the speed of light far behind, where for example, comunication between here and the moon appears to be instantaneous. The inventor described below proved that to the U.S. National Aeronautics and Space Agency (NASA), but that information was "buried".

In about 1946, a free-thinking American inventor by the name of T. Galen Hyeronemous invented a strange frequency based system, and follow - through devices which would lead to a serious number of other new discoveries and phenomena.

My source of the information concerning that series of discoveries and inventions, was a soft cover book by Joseph Goodavage, called "Magic, Science of the Future".

Of the books Joseph Goodavage wrote and had published, (and there were a few of them), this particular book was not listed in the U.S. Library of Congress index of books and authors that we checked out in California in 1993. My guess is that it was stricken from that list. It only had one publishing run, and no further editions were published, even though the book was very fascinating to me, and revealing in the areas of psychic communications and inventions related to those subjects. Funny that should happen. Perhaps our controllers did not want any of that information to get out or to become public knowledge. (PSI frequencies penetrate cloaking invisibility systems, so "cloaked" craft can be seen and identified. That is the probable reason for suppression, at a deeper level.) Cloaking is dimensional change, and PSI frequencies are multi-dimensional.

My wife and I looked around for copies of that book a few months later. She eventually found only 2 copies in used book stores. This effort covered the region from San Diego California, to Salt Lake City, and proceeded north to Victoria, British Columbia, and then east to Calgary. This does not leave out the cities in between. I can remember checking out used book stores in Las Vegas, Reno, L.A., San Francisco, Seattle, etc., on the way back north.

What I am suggesting here, is that psychic communication is totally real, and is a universal reality, not just a local phenomena. It also operates within a specific frequency range. Most of our extraterrestrial friends are capable of telepathic communication. They communicate with systems based on that range of frequencies, to be able to contact us. It is logical that if they broadcast to you or me on that frequency, with enough intensity, we will easily get the message.

It appears that our "secret controllers" wanted this technology to be suppressed and not made available to the rest of us, who might find out that they were not all that smart, powerful or omnipotent, and should not be in control of our destiny?

Incidentally, our controllers have been using this technology themselves for quite a number of years as reported by the "CONTACT" newspaper, some time ago.

Our Evolution - "Conventional" Points of View & Logical Observations:

We are at the outer fringe of the Pleiades star cluster. That is why we observe so many other neighboring constellations and star clusters which are easily seen from our perspective. We are not looking through the two thousand or more stars in our own star cluster, as we are at its outer fringe with a clearer view outward and up and down relative to our constellation of Taurus.

Our astronomers and astrophysicists have said that since we are out at the fringe of the star system we are in, our solar system is a comparatively young system, and we have not had much time to evolve.

I think that assumption could be B.S. and there are two rather good reasons why my thinking is a little different. Firstly, if this universe and Galaxy are constantly expanding, one would think the most recent evolution would be back to the center of the universe and of the galaxy, whichever we are referring to, and ours should be one of the older sentient races. Another bothersome observation: I tend to think of the "big bang theory" as perhaps being related to a strong laxative, which should be applied to those who support that theory.

Secondly, if we consider human progress in the past thousand years, and that we have advanced in the last two hundred years from sailing ships to spacecraft, there surely is a problem with so-called conventional thinking. At the rate we are presently going, we should be out there exploring the rest of the galaxy, easily within the next 50+- years. That is, if we can get rid of the parasitic bastards who are presently controlling us and our progress toward anything other than our enslavement under their own dictatorial control.

It seems ridiculous to assume that we are that backward and stupid. Is it just a matter of our so-called scientists thinking that they are the only "rare" smart ones among us, even if it is not usually those folks who come up with the new ideas and technology? They sure as hell do not create conceptually new inventions as often as they should, if they are so damn smart. Copy cat technology is their specialty. However, among them there are large numbers of very good teachers, and they are exceptionally important to our progress. Those who are good teachers are usually not as smug and self important as others I have met.

Our Arrival, With Evolution Completed:
Our friends in the Galactic Federation, more recently, and certain gifted and implanted individuals as well, going back to the 1970's, have been telling us a different story about our earliest beginnings on this planet. Our so-called "elite" controlling group of greedy self serving criminals do not want us to know any of the real truth about our beginnings. Their continuing efforts toward keeping us ignorant and maintaining absolute control since the time of Atlantis, is also not supposed to be known or revealed to us.

Our major publishers, as owned and / or controlled by our Luciferian dark side folks since as early as 1954, have published very little information that has had any real meaning, or anything but speculative academic crap, concerning that matter.

They have avoided psychic sources as well. Once you get a look at the truth, you will find that Darwin's theory of Evolution doesn't quite fit our own real pattern of development. Also, there is the matter of genetic alteration, which the Galactic Federation folks say was well and completely known and developed by sentient races in this galaxy millions of years ago.

Our forbears, as far as the ancient continent of Lemuria, in the middle of the Pacific Ocean was concerned, originally came from the third planet in the Sirius B solar system. That planet is called "Akonowai". Doesn't that sound interesting, when we relate it to the language of the Hawaiians? It also directly and clearly relates to the language pattern of the rest of the Polynesians.

In case you are wondering about the skin color of our Hawaiian and other Polynesian folks in the Pacific islands are brown, that is no real indication to be dealing with. The skin color of the Sirians from the Sirius B solar system is either white or light blue. It has been explained in writings I have come across in the past 30 years or so, that after our "firmament" was collapsed, which caused the "flood", the damaging rays of the sun changed the skin color of the blue race to shades of brown. We now have light and medium brown to almost black, depending on the intensity of the sun in a particular region of this planet.

THE FIRMAMENT:

Now is the time to explain what was meant by the firmament, as mentioned in the bible. Most other occupied planets in this galaxy have a firmament. A firmament is either one, two or three layers of ice crystals surrounding a planet, at an altitude of 15,000 ft. to 40,000 ft. What the firmament does in each and all cases, as long as it remains intact, is to block off and disperse the most damaging frequencies from the star (or sun) involved, in each case, so that the DNA of its sentient occupants is not damaged to any extent. The previous existence of a firmament on this planet is why Abraham and his family are said to have had life spans in the order of 750 to 900 years.

With our sun we are dealing with an extremely powerful fusion reaction, having been a hydrogen fusion reaction, with perhaps some minor variations, until recently. As we compare the color variations in various stars out there in the cosmos there are large numbers of similar situations. Among those marvelously powerful rays of sustaining energy, some frequencies can be extremely damaging. Our sun is now said to have a helium fusion reaction, and its light is now more white and intense, and could be more damaging to our bodies.

Further to our comments concerning the Polynesians, It has also been explained that the most predominant group to colonize other smaller parts of this planet with white skinned folks were the Pleiadeans. They, along with the white skinned folks from Sirius B are the forebears of what we would call the strongly white skinned Aryan racial groups.

In the last few thousand years the white bloodlines from the Pleiades would have been dominant, because they came here more recently in our ancient history. Historically, as to our present world, the whites were originally in Iran, then as they migrated to other regions, becoming everything from Hebrews to Northern Germans to Scandinavians. It is surely interesting to note that one of the main Pleiadean languages resembles German.

Are you now wondering about the Orientals, thinking of the Chinese in particular? Actually, the Galactic Federation representative, "Washta" from Sirius B, has explained that original immigrants to this planet who eventually became the Chinese, and evolved through interbreeding, into a series of other related far eastern groups, came here from Andromeda. The basics of the Chinese language and related dialects are also said to have come from that source.

In the case of the earlier CONTACT newspaper, virtually all of the so-called dictated material, over a period of about 11 years was transmitted directly to the recipient by means of a special short wave based system which beamed the information directly to the mind of the recipient. Those folks were usually the Plieadians. In the case of material received and published by Sheldan Nidle, a similar broadcasting system was being used by the Sirians. The difference, however, is that in Sheldan's case; he had been implanted by the Sirians, when he was a child, with a multi-dimensional crystal receiver.

Both of those systems involve direct communication which eliminates individualized opinions and re-wording, resulting in a very clear message or teaching effort or whatever, to come across, and to be printed out accordingly.

CHAPTER 5

DUMBING DOWN THE HUMAN RACE

Even though you will certainly not find it unless you look for it, there is a rather complete story of how the human race was "dumbed down", and relegated to the level of slaves to an elite group of controllers. This took place on Atlantis. That has been further confirmed in the book, "Your Galactic Neighbors" by Sheldan Nidle, as previously mentioned, and other sources which I have accessed in the past 20 years.

The Atlantean "royalty" were mesmerized by a certain fellow of extreme capability, called "Lucifer", who is said to be a spiritual brother of his opposite, the personage who has since become known as "Jmanuel", "Esu Ben Joseph", and much later, Jesus of Nazareth., or Jesus the "Christ".

In reality, any person attaining the level of an "ascended master" is the equivalent of a "Christed one". Once you catch up in the "what was going on" department, it is surprising what many of the "half truths" in the bible have been really saying or alluding to, in spite of our momentary lack of understanding.

In any event, what is said to have really happened, is that the Atlantean royalty, given the reptilian model of government as an example, accepted the idea that they could become supreme virtual deities in their empire, and eventually this entire planet. They agreed that steps could then be taken to achieve that objective. Lucifer's "helpers", originally from the Sirius star system, had some assistance from people and a lady in particular, from the Centaurus system, very highly developed by that time, and only 4.39 light years from Earth.

Government at that time by Lucifer and his gang was based on the form of government, then existing throughout the Anchara Alliance of reptilian civilizations stretching from Saggitarius to Draco, to Orion, and infringing on our own neighbourhood. Lucifer and his followers set up a government with regions, where each region had its King, and a series of Earls, Counts, etc., as common in medieval Europe. That type of government was chosen as it is really the only type that can achieve and maintain total control over its citizens, by a small number of "elite" individuals.

The form of government, based on kings at the top, dukes etc., on the way down, and we, the peasants at the bottom, is the way things are in this world at the present time. Most of us do not realize that controlling corporations are the manipulators within this "modern" system of things. The elite types at the top are not quite ready to concede their lofty positions. They would not concede that in Atlantis, until Atlantis sunk into the sea. - Then they buzzed off to Centaurus.

Many of the controllers went to the bottom along with most of the ordinary citizens. Our situation looks somewhat similar at the present time.

Things moved along in Atlantis until genetic alteration was completed as planned, where the intelligence and sentience of us ordinary human beings on this planet was reduced to 3 on a scale of 10. Our extraterrestrial brothers have a mental level of 8 to 10, and we now have, on the average, a mental level of 3. Our genetics were also altered to make us desire a "leader", and that desire, in a high percentage of us became something like an "obsession". Darn good system for controlling us, which has worked rather well so far . . .

The Atlantean leaders of that era wanted to gain total enslavement control over this planet. Other empires, including China (Yu), Egypt, and a very scientifically advanced one (Ionia), which would now be northern Greece, were totally opposed to the imperialistic expansion plans of the Atlanteans. A series of wars began at that time, which continued for another 5,000 years.

Eventually, about 6,000 years ago, a war between Atlantis and the dissenting kingdoms was fought, with devastating results. Anti-gravity discoid aircraft, rocket propelled bombs, and things of that nature were part of that scenario. If you take the time and opportunity to read the "VEDAS", those craft and their weapons are described. Isn't that interesting?

When things got really tenuous, one of the kingdoms decided to collapse the firmament. (They thought it would only be partial...) That resulted in 40 days and 40 nights of rain, now known as "the flood". The entire surface of the planet changed in that short period of time, and "civilization" went to hell in a hand basket. The elite "controllers" from Atlantis then took off and went to a planet in a solar system in the area of our closest star neighbor, Centaurus, where some of those Atlantean controllers had come from, a long time before.

The reptilian leadership did not let their subjects know anything about what they were planning or doing. That has completely been the case as well, on this planet, since those times. - A reptilian form of government. Some of their devious lying human types, known as the "illuminati" have been trying to finalize the process of setting up a worldwide "slave state" system of things. Their current plan began to evolve about 6000 years ago, not long after the flood.

The close by reptilian hybrids, as mentioned above are the "Annunaki", and they occupy a large water planet called "Nibiru", which orbits around Sirius B, in a very long orbit. Nibiru swings in our direction, passing through our solar system once every 3,600 years. It is referred to as "wormwood" in the bible.

Going back to the Atlantean situation in its time, those scientists carefully blocked the etheric or spiritual energy field connections to 10 of the 12 strands of our DNA. That left us with the following limitations compared to the perpetrators of that situation:

1.)   Our intelligence level in a comparative sense dropped to a 2.5 to 3.0 on the average, based on a scale of 10, as related to the folks from Sirius and Centaurus, for instance.

2.)   Our previously quite common natural abilities of clair-voyance, clairaudience, telekinesis, and holographic mental visualization all but disappeared in a general sense, with only the occasional one of us having a strong ability in any of the senses they were then eliminating.

(To clarify the matter of "Holographic mental imaging" and to what extent it remains in spite of those precursors of the illuminati, most of us conceptual inventors, including me have retained or recovered some of that ability.)

3.)   Even more restricting, we totally manipulated humans were also instilled with a very keen desire to require a leader or leaders to tell us what to think and do, and we would always want a leader, and not take the initiative ourselves.

Have you observed that the ones (politicians) who would or did take the initiative, have ended up being a corruptible bunch of crooks most of the time? Those idiots were also looking for leaders and found them, in our own time frame. In examining that situation, the dark side of the equation has its representatives in positions of power, and that has certainly been the case for a long time.

Although some of the above limitations have been reduced in some of us who have been more fortunate, they remain generally true for a very large proportion of our present population.

Even though, in the broader sense, that entire set of limitations has sustained itself, throughout the general population, there have always been exceptions. Since the time of Moses, the human race gradually began to recover some of its spiritual gifts and abilities. This had been arranged originally by the Pleiadeans, and later enhanced at any time they could do so, by the Sirians.

An upward universal frequency and energy field change is now well under way in the lower dimensions, including the one we occupy, and that has begun to remove those limitations. Our DNA is progressively repairing itself, and we Earth humans are moving upward in intelligence. Many of us will also regain and begin to experience some of those lost or suppressed psychic abilities.

The Annunaki were a quietly dominant factor in the larger scheme of things concerning their most recent 6,000 years of involvement on Earth. They created and later continued to control and direct the "Illuminati" who began as human/reptilian hybrids, and have been our direct secret government controllers for the last two thousand years in particular. It is interesting to note that in the case of Roman coins, those made 2,000 years ago show the 8 pointed star as a main symbol. The 8 pointed star is the symbol of Nibiru, the home planet of the Annunaki.

I will now fill you in on the reptilians, and try to make it as short as possible, without writing another book. Firstly, the reptilians as a broadly based species first appeared in our sector of the galaxy as immigrants from the constellation of Sagittarius, to the constellation of Draco, about 35 million years ago.

The ultimate leader, motivator and Deity of the Reptilians was a manifestation of Satan, in a female format, and was addressed and referred to as "Anchara". Anchara required that the reptilians become the fiercest warriors, warmongers and destroyers in the galaxy. Anchara gave them the mandate to proceed to conquer and occupy and/or destroy any and all other civilizations in the galaxy that were not reptilian, or subservient to Anchara. This mandate represented the negative side of our negative and positive universe of Nebadon, which has also been referred to as "Orvonton".

God provided that all beings incarnated in this universe would be in a duality of negative and positive, and the grand experiment was to eventually have the positive or love side of things end up winning over the negative side. Even the book of Revelation in the bible lays out this situation. We are now in the end times, and certain events as predicted therein are now taking place.

The Reptilians had a religion and philosophy which dictated that they, as a species were to be supreme in this galaxy. They assumed or decided that they should eradicate all other sentient species which might compete with them in any way toward becoming dominant in this galaxy. = <u>Satan & Lucifer.</u>

The next area that they conquered and occupied as part of their evil empire was part of the Constellation of Orion, much closer to us, about 25 million years ago.

Over millions of years since, the main governing system for many sectors of the galaxy in this particular region, was the Bellatrix solar system, in the constellation of Orion. As far as our planet Earth is concerned, the first time they destroyed a human civilization on this planet was when they destroyed the civilization known as Hybornia, a couple of million years ago, and at the same time, they devastated the surfaces of Mars and Venus.

In the meantime, after that, the Galactic Federation, with headquarters for this sector being located on Sirius B, were keeping our solar system under observation. Reptilian control of our solar system would put the reptilians in a very close strategic position if they wanted to attack any member planets of the Federation in this sector. Almost all of the planetary systems in this region were then occupied by humans.

As stated in the "Vedas", the ancient written history of India, there is a series of cycles in this universe. Our galaxy and the local constellation of stars in which we exist, will experience the consequences of the currently happening change in the scheme of things, whether we like it or not. The Vedas have said that one complete orbital cycle of this galaxy is 206 million years. Guess what? We are now there... (The Convergence - August 17th., 1987 was said to be that date..)

Galactic Cycles, Dimensionality, & Our Fast-Changing World:

Our controllers do not want us to know or contemplate these things. The main consequence of the completion of each orbital cycle of this galaxy is an upward movement in frequency and dimensionality. Sounds fine if we don't know the difference. However, an upward step in dimensionality is also a clear difference in solidity, comprehension and existence at large. If you are not spiritually aware to a certain level, you will not be able to either comprehend the upward change in frequency, or be able to physically tolerate it.

In view of the previous statement, what if you cannot physically tolerate the frequency change and related upward dimensional movement? You would be transferred to another 3rd. dimensional planet and related environment, to continue your evolution toward oneness with our creator. Time is said to be not a problem, or even a serious consideration in the 5th. Dimension. In the third dimension it appears to be the key framework of our entire existence.

It seems to me that the linear value of time varies in direct proportion to changes in frequency. As we have moved upward in frequency toward the 5th Dimension, time has moved forward so fast, that it seemed to have shortened considerably.

Have you noticed that "phenomenon"? You sure have done so, if you are a normal human in the present scheme of things, and not an ascended master, where it probably does not matter. I have surely noticed that phenomena and other thinking persons in my area have also noticed that. Those who do not think much usually do not notice very much. (Time is almost zero in the 5th dimension.)

Now, let's give you something else to think about... All dimensions of reality relate to frequency. I personally think, after making countless observations, that time is directly proportional to dimensionality. Our 3rd.dimensional time is a long, slow and arduous process. In the higher dimensions, time tends to shrink in our terms to where it is not quite so noticeable. This would be somewhat like electricity and magnetism being 90 degrees opposed on a 2-dimensional plane, and 180 degrees opposed on a 3-dimensional plane, with geometry coming into play, and our "educated" thinkers telling us that dimensions are individual planes and then multiple planes of progressively complex and expanding geometric structure. Time could also be proportionately cyclical within a particular dimension. That is my observation at this time. The Montauk Project proved 20-year time cycles in 3D. Chapter 19 and page 83 will relate to these things as well.

Now, consider that you and me, and all others around us that we see within our framework, are in a particular frequency pattern which defines our presence and existence. Most humans seem to think that the frequency band containing our own framework is all that there is. There is nothing wrong with that. If we think about it, we might assume that our existence may only be possible within a certain narrow range, or frequency band within a far broader containment. Could there be a much larger range of frequencies which might represent a progressive series of different realities?

In case you might be wondering what criteria might have determined whether or not time was related to frequency, I will try to bring you up-to-date. What I have to say may stimulate you. It has already been proven, somewhat by surprise that fooling around with dimensionality momentarily cancels out time...

I will now bring you back down to our ordinary world, where the action began in the U.S. in 1943, and continued there to

1986, and for some time after that, as time cycles repeated themselves in our misunderstood reality. (started in Germany, in 1941+-, continued by the nazis in the U.S., & financed by the nazis in Germany.) – Ashkenazi ? – Does that add up ?

It is a fact that the Germans had already built and tested sequential and progressively improved models of anti-gravity flying craft, and had their last and best model with spaceship capability by the end of World War Two. It should also be borne in mind that probably 75% of the top scientists engineers and technicians, particularly if they belonged to the SS, were quietly "rescued" by the U.S. from Germany. They were provided with new technical positions, and even new names if required, by the secret nazi groups behind the U.S. government. The Germans were also very close to detonation capability with their nuclear bomb technology by the end of World War Two. The SS took over the CIA, at the action end of the American fascist secret government.

If the statements immediately above were a bit bothersome to your own perspectives, that information is available, partly on http://www.rense.com , with further references and details in the CONTACT newspaper and the Phoenix Journals, with odd references also having been made in books such as "Beyond Top Secret" and a couple of others in the last 10 years. The Rense source has a series of diagrams and photos. Those flying saucers were called variously "Vril" and "Vimanas" by the Germans, Pleiadeans, and in the ancient Vedas of India.

Time Machines??

Away back in 1945-46, we totally controlled humans were absolutely unaware of our unscrupulous masters and their controlling schemes. At the end of World War 2, a few things happened which resulted in the establishment of a special project which was set up on Long Island in the state of New York. A train, carrying multi-millions of dollars in Gold, was hijacked by being stopped in a tunnel in Europe, immediately after the end of World War 2.

It is interesting to note, but never was published, that 50+ American military personnel, guarding that train, carrying the Gold, were murdered. The Gold had been hijacked by the German SS, and was later placed on a submarine, for delivery to a secret location. It was **Montauk Point**, on Long Island in the State of New York. Technology provided by E.T.'s to our secret rulers led to "new technology". The Germans had already developed and tested a time machine, which was working before the end of World War II. Its further development, and deployment was considered important by our then quickly evolving One World Order. (They were always tied back to the German SS; and based on all of the police state legislation now in place in the U.S. it could be referred to as "The Fourth Reich". Virtually all of their main principals and financiers were in the U.S. (The "Bush" banking family and others). The Montauk project had been pre-planned, and the Gold was stolen toward secretly funding the longer term development of the time machine technology.

By the time the **Montauk Project** had begun, the **Philadelphia Experiment** had been carried out. A space-time warp had been created & experienced in the Philadelphia Experiment, where a number of participants (military, of lower rank) were either caught in between solidity and space, by being locked into steel plate, etc., or moving on into the next dimension, and then returning, when the power was turned off. Other than those who did not survive, some of the crew that did survive became mentally deranged.

It was also reported, that when some of those non-commissioned officers who had survived went to bars etc., they found they could walk through doors and walls...

What the principles involved in the experiment were learning, was that space and time are more directly related, and at a more elementary level, in this dimension, than they had theorized. Even though key persons involved at the scientific level with the Philadelphia Experiment were not aware of it, their controllers at a higher level, had learned that the space/time situation would be consequential to the Experiment, and a serious problem to be dealt with. Now, let's continue with the Montauk Project, in more specific terms.

The German time machine technology had the potential of moving them toward control of time. They really wanted to control everything and everybody else to begin with, and it is no surprise that they would set up the Montauk Project in 1945, toward achieving that objective.

The Montauk Project was successful, being that movies were taken of the past, back more than 250,000 years, and into the future for about 9,000 + years. In the 1980's they did a VCR movie of the crucifixion of Christ, and a few other rather important historical events in our history, as we know it. All of that is bearing in mind that the past is done and solid, and the future can, and is based on probabilities related to our own thoughts and actions which influence and define those probabilities.

As a further point of interest, as earlier mentioned, they also found out that time runs in 20 year cycles, and any point in the past could then be most easily accessed at any exactly 20 year incremental point, since that earlier point in time. That is why the time point of the Philadelphia Experiment was accessed by the Montauk Project in 1983, 40 years after the date of the experiment.

At the present moment, that 20 year cycle may be no longer valid, as our ambient dimensional frequency is already more like the 4th. Dimension, rather than the 3rd, and I cannot imagine that not affecting the time cycle.

If you find this fascinating, look up the book "The Montauk Project". The author, or one of them, is Al Bielek. It is a very interesting book. If you have a scientific mind, it will be specially fascinating, as it also covers further frequency experiments related to mind control, involving both humans & animals. As I remember, there were also some early weather control experiments, based on technology stolen from Wilhelm Reich. Reich had earlier been jailed on trumped up charges, and had died in jail. **(That was another murder that I had not mentioned, as having been done by the CIA and/or the secret government.)**

It is seriously bothersome to realize that those controllers could have such complete control of such large numbers of us, and not have to worry about how many they kidnapped or killed, as they proceeded with their projects. If you read the book, that will be apparent. Thousands of young folks were kidnapped, and used in the time tunnel experiments. Many of them were lost without being able to come back.

The time machine technology was seriously developed, and has been put to use on many occasions. I am also aware from other written sources that our extraterrestrial friends and neighbors had developed and learned how to use time machines a very long time ago. They can make good use of that technology any time it is convenient for them to do so, without erasing their total existence in the process. However, within our present framework, and beginning at a much earlier point in time, they have remained honor bound not to interfere with the evolution or progress of any other sentient beings in this universe.

Aside from the reptilians, including the Annunaki directors of the Illuminati, the Galactic Federation has kept to that set of ground rules. The Annunaki abandoned the Illuminati in the mid-1990's when they joined the Federation. The Illuminati have continued their nefarious actions on their own, ever since that time.

It must be borne in mind that from our present perspective, the past is a solid issue, if we use a time machine to access the past. The future is not the same. The future consists of a number of possibilities, and what we get in a future projection will not necessarily turn out to be what we have accessed with our time machine. (Our thought projections define our future.)

Here is the kicker. You might be fascinated with the idea of going back in time to see a real picture of what happened in a certain era. That is all well and good. However, if you venture into the future, you are going into the realm of probabilities, which is just as real as a concept, as anything else you have observed so far... Then, unless you are just checking out next week, or the day after tomorrow, how certain can you be? (Unified Field & Particle Physics).

It has been said that the future takes shape on the basis of the composite of the thought projections of all of us involved in a particular time line, as we move toward any future point in time. I have read that explanation as presented by at least three other sources, and cannot suggest that I am smart enough to provide any better description of what really happens.

The only thing I can see that is really most important about using a time machine is that we could go backward with real certainty and determine what our real history was, rather than having to believe the bullshit imposed upon us by our controllers. Based on what our extraterrestrial friends have recently said, the real truth is _very_ different from what they have been telling us.

Chapter 6

OTHER CIVILIZATIONS IN OUR REGION OF
THE MILKY WAY GALAXY

A person, who is an author and does public speaking engagements concerning our Galactic Neighbors and any and all related subjects, has written a number of fascinating books. This person's name is Sheldan Nidle. He was born and raised in the state of New York. He has had constant contacts with the Sirians, particularly as they represent the Galactic Federation.

Sheldan was equipped with physical and etheric implants at a very early age, and has been able, ever since, to receive directly, rather than psychically, very accurate and complete communications from the Sirians. They have provided a massive amount of information to him over the past 50+ years, and much of it has now been published.

Our totally controlled media can't stop this completely and accurately reported information, and are at a loss to do anything about it. I think that is really marvelous, as so much of the information I have had to chase down for the previous 40 years had to come from other more private publishing sources, and also, in some cases, private and used book stores, all across the western half of North America.

A great deal of what I am about to reveal or relate to you, concerning our Galactic neighbors comes from a book by Sheldan Nidle called "Your Galactic Neighbors". I seriously and personally recommend that you should obtain your own copy of that marvelous book. I have now bought my second copy. The first one was mislaid at Dorval airport at Montreal, when I was on the way to Italy on a business trip in October of 2006. I had been busy studying all of the marvelous other folks in this sector of the galaxy, including humans, reptilians, cetaceans, amphibians, and equines. All of their civilizations are vastly more advanced than ours, and all of them can zoom across the galaxy at speeds that meet or exceed 35 light years per minute.

Mother told me, as a child, that most of my limitations were self-imposed and my attitude and self-confidence were far more important. Perhaps our scientific establishment should begin to adopt that kind of thinking, as well. We need to leap out of our more modern version of the Stone Age, PDQ, so we can at least begin to understand and appreciate our more advanced galactic neighbors.

Please access Sheldan Nidle's website: http://www.paoweb. com. to get his current updates or to order copies of his fascinating books, including the marvelous one I have mentioned above. Sheldan Nidle, in his books as mostly dictated to him by our Sirian friends, representing the Galactic Federation, has provided most of the carefully condensed information that I am about to reveal to you concerning our Galactic Neighbors. Sheldan's books are far more detailed, to the point of providing drawings and general descriptions of ET craft, Equines, Amphibians and Cetaceans.

I strongly recommend that you buy his books and read them to complete your coverage of what our galactic neighborhood is all about. You will learn about many of the marvelous species of highly sentient beings in our sector who are traveling throughout this galaxy and beyond. Sheldan's Planetary Activation Organization has been set up by himself, with background suggestions and support from our Galactic Federation friends. This organization is to prepare us for becoming Galactic Humans in a wide awake fashion. This is directly related to our presently increasing ambient (dimensional) frequency, which incidentally, is now said (in 2007) to have already reached 5th. Dimensional level.

The closest primarily human civilization to us is in the Centaurus star cluster. Its closest human occupied planet is only 4.39 light years from us. The Galactic Federation refers to the constellation of Centaurus as the great star union of

Centaurus. It represents hundreds of star nations of both humans and human / reptilian hybrids. The first Star or planetary system is referred to as Proxima Centauri, which is a triple star system. Rigel Centaurus, one of the triple stars in this closest system to us, was first colonized by humans from the constellation of Lyra, nearly 2.5 million years ago. On the planet referred to as Endo, one of the larger water worlds in the Proxima Centauri system, its oceans have whales larger than those of Earth.

Human Centaurians strongly resemble Earth humans. However, they are much taller than us. Males range from 6 to 8 feet in height, and females range from 5 feet 5 inches to 7 feet in height. Centaurian hair is brown, black or red. Skin color is either very dark brown or tan. Eyes, either almond shaped or round are black, brown green or hazel.

The reptilian Centaurian is very scaly, lizardly and muscular, with variegated skin, either blue and green or red and green. The eyes are round and bulging, with vertical slits in either red or gold. Their hands, narrower than those of a human have 6 fingers, and end in very sharp curved claws. There is no tail. The female is slightly taller than the male, with a height of just under 8 feet. These folks are very advanced by our human standards and only need 2 to 4 hours of sleep per day.

Before we get carried away with interstellar distances from Earth, we must consider that those distances don't mean much, where the fully evolved civilizations out there have spacecraft that can travel at or exceeding a speed of 35 light years per minute. What I am getting at, is that we should not get hung up with our scientists silly limitations, which really do not apply to the other folks out there.

We have been learning at a prodigious rate for the last 500 years. Those folks with 3 times our intelligence have obviously learned a great deal more than us in the last 2 to 4 million years.

I am at a loss to figure out what makes our present species of scientist so darn smart that they are constantly defining our "limitations". I personally feel that it is only "their own" limitations that they are referring to. Those of us humans who are non-linear and creative do not attach to any personal limitations, pre-conceived or otherwise, as a general rule, unless we prefer not to jump out of our boxes.

We Humans Are Smaller Than Those Humans–How Come?

In order to understand and appreciate why most of us Earth humans are much shorter in height than our genetically close relatives out there, there is a clear explanation for that situation. At the end of the last great conflict, fought between Atlantis, and China, and the other great landmass which is now India, and Tibet, the great conflagration referred to as the flood was caused by the Atlanteans, and forerunners of the Illuminati, as they were being defeated at the time, and would sooner destroy all civilization than lose the ability to enslave the rest of its population. Our present moment in time is certainly not any different, or haven't you noticed?

The Chinese and a scientific rebel group originally from the Atlantis royalty, who wanted to stop Atlantis from enslaving the rest of the world, had decided the Atlanteans had to be stopped. This advanced civilization (Ionia) was not far from what would be referred to as Greece at the present time. When the Atlanteans attacked, the scientific rebel group was joined by Rama, a powerful king or chieftain, from the inner world civilization of Agartha, which then had discoid craft and advanced technology, at least a match for that of the Atlanteans.

Anyway, if you ever get a chance to look into the Vedas, the ancient history books of the people of India, who are largely descended from Rama's blood lines, you will read that a great conflict took place away back in time. Some have said that was 8,000 years ago. Our galactic neighbors place that time at about 13,000 years ago. You will find that the discoid anti gravity flying craft of the Agarthans were referred to as "Vimanas", and rocket propelled missiles are also mentioned. I cannot say those missiles had nuclear warheads, but if they did, they were of our "more modern" low yield type. It is interesting to note that the Pleiadeans still refer to some of their older model discoid scout ships as Vimanas, in case you are still thinking about where our dominant languages came from, and if you read the VEDAS, they are called just that.

You will also note that the Old Testament mentions the "firmament", with reference to the flood. What had happened, is that certain pyramid types and crystal towers had been set up thousands of years earlier, and acted as a solid state type of frequency-based support system, which held up our firmament.

The firmament consisted of two protective layers of ice crystals, with one being at about 15,000 to 18,000 ft., and the other at about 35,000 to 38,000 ft. up. What the firmament achieved was the blockage, back reflection or dispersal of the most damaging rays of our sun. That is why, away back at the time of Adam, and until the firmament was destroyed, our Earth humans were much taller than we are now, and much closer in height to our galactic neighbors from the Pleiades and Sirius in particular, our strongest genetic forebears.

Also, as you might remember, when you read about Adam and Abraham, you will find that our human life span in those days was 750 to 950 years.

With reference to Adam, the most recently recovered scrolls (4 of them), with the writings of Judas Iscariot, who was Jesus' scribe. They say that Adam's father came from what our astronomers refer to as the 7 Sisters being the 7 other stars in the Pleiadean star cluster that our ill-equipped astronomers can commonly recognize. Our sun is said to be the 8th star in our star group, within the constellation of

Taurus.

Pardon me for continuing to bring up these other odd things. However, in sometimes small and yet important ways, these other odds and ends add together to complete a story, with fewer dead ends and unexplained details.

Some Star Nations Described In "Your Galactic Neighbors" - With A Brief Summary of Each:

A.)   Mostly or Exclusively Human:

1.) Andromeda:
Andromeda is a very large constellation, ranging from 150 to 400 light years from Earth. Andromedans are known throughout the galaxy as great scientists and healers. They have been members of the Galactic Federation of Light for about 3.5 million years. Andromedan home worlds range from water planets similar to Earth, to semi-arid realms, more hospitable to reptilians.

Andromedans resemble Earth humans in appearance. The first type is a Caucasian, with features varying from so-called Nordic (blond hair, blue eyes & pale skin), to a Mediterranean type, with dark brown hair, grey to brown eyes, and tanned looking skin. The second type is typically Asian, with dark hair, dark almond shaped eyes and brown skin that can vary in color from very pale to dark brown. The eyes of all Andromedans are a little larger than those of Earth humans. Their thin lips are very pale pink, while the ears are fitted slightly lower on the side of the head and are somewhat smaller in size. Their hands and feet are delicate in appearance with long fingers and toes.

Although the fully sentient beings in the Andromeda constellation are heavily on the human side, there appears to be an exception. Our Equine neighbors in the Arcturus system have said that they originally evolved there, and came from

Andromeda, millions of years ago, before colonizing Arcturus. Also typically, it is very likely that there are some other sentient species of interest that we have not been told about, to keep the story from getting too elaborate.

2.) Altair:

Altair (Alpha Aquila) is the brightest star in the constellation of Aquila. The Altarians are primarily a humanoid species, with a few reptilian and dinosaurian hybrids living among them. The Altarians resemble us in many ways, despite some major differences.

Regardless of gender, the average Altarian stands over 7 feet tall. Their skin is naturally very smooth and hairless, and that is primarily referring to the fact that they don't grow a beard, or have facial hair etc. (neither did our Atlanteans, as a primary blood line, and presently, the purer blood lines among our North American Indians also may not have or grow a beard or even pubic hair.)

The Altarians' skin tones range from very pale white, to those of the average European. Their eyes, unlike ours, are large and recognizable for their round or almond shape. Most often they are sapphire blue, but occasionally green or yellow. The nose is either large and aquiline or small and slightly bulbous. Their lips are extremely thin and their canine teeth are large. Their ears are delicate and somewhat larger than ours. Hair is thick and blond, red or brown-black. These interesting folks have libraries of knowledge going back for about 25 million years.

If you attempted to relate the Altarians back to our own lineage of humanoid, you would come to a dead end, perhaps 8 million years ago. It would appear to me that the Altarians probably evolved from a different and much earlier primary lineage.

3.) Epsilon Eridani:

Epsilon Eridani was first colonized from Sirius B, and later by a large contingent of colonists from the constellation of Andromeda.

Located between Orion and Taurus, Epsilon Eridani is about 10.5 light years from Earth, near the middle of the constellation of Eridanus.

Its third planet, with 6 continents has a surface area that is about 70% water, with deep oceans. Its fourth planet has a surface area of only about 50% water, and is a drier planet with much landscape similar to our Sahara desert. Both of those planets are populated.

Epsilon Eridani has been a member of the Galactic Federation of Light for about 3.7 million years, and is a member of the Sirian Federation Regional Council. Earth's representatives will soon become active members of this regional council. Epsilon Eridani humans mostly resemble their original Sirius B human colonists. Men's bodies vary from perfectly formed muscular physiques to child-like builds, and range from 6 feet 6 inches to 7 feet 4 inches in height. Hair is blonde to light brown and eyes are light blue to green. Women are extremely voluptuous and stand between 6 feet 2 inches and 6 feet 8 inches in height. Epsilon Eridani skin tones are extremely pale, light red or light blue. Like their Sirian relatives they require only about 2 hours of sleep per day.

Larger Space Ships (Mother Ships):

The largest mother ships from Epsilon Eridani have a lozenge shaped main hull, 4000 miles long, surrounded by, and tube connected to a group of smaller lozenges. I just wanted you to get a feel for how big some of the mother ships of some of the nations in this galaxy really are. The largest mother ship mentioned in "Your Galactic Neighbors" is a reptilian mother ship from Sigma Draconis. It and a couple of others mentioned therein are much larger than 4000 miles long or across. That is almost beyond the imagination of any of us Earth humans, when our planet is only about 7,900 miles in diameter.

Before we start with any general descriptions of Alpha Aries and its human citizens, here is a very pertinent and interrelated issue that motivated much migration and colonization of this sector of the galaxy. We are speaking of migrations to this region by people from the older human civilizations in the constellations of Lyra, Sirius, Andromeda and in our Pleiades star cluster in the constellation of Taurus.

Away back in time, the Alpha Aries solar system was one of a series of strategic defense colonies set up by the Galactic Federation of Light, to defend against incessant forays by reptilians from Orion and Draco, in particular. The reptilians (Anchara Alliance of Reptilian Empires - the "Dark Side") began the process at least 25 million years ago, of attacking and either destroying or subjugating planets in all other solar systems then occupied by sentient beings other than reptilians. Please bear in mind that there are hundreds of thousands of occupied solar systems in our own small sector of this galaxy, with some constellations containing as many as 2000 solar systems.

The Galactic Federation of Light began to be led and dominated by their more advanced humans as far back as 5 to 6 million years ago, when the main headquarters of the Federation was already in existence in the constellation of Lyra, in the planetary system of Vega. The humans quickly began, and have continued to push the reptilians back into their own territory ever since. This was achieved with the valued assistance of certain land based cetaceans in particular, and further by placing human defense type colonies at strategic points along the periphery of then Federation controlled territory, and moving outward as it expanded.

It should also be mentioned here, that the Book of Revelation in the Bible, mentions that the dark side would be conquered, or go over to the light, and that we would then have a "thousand years of peace". In that context, it is interesting to note that Anchara, the god or spiritual leader of the reptilians announced to the reptilians in 1994, that "now" was the time for peace.

The reptilians were told that they should proceed to join the Galactic Federation, toward achieving peace throughout this galaxy. Virtually all of the reptilian star nations, thousands of them, all the way from Sagittarius, to Draco, to Orion, along with scattered smaller groups in our closer constellations and star clusters have now joined their local regional council of the Galactic Federation, in such a short time, since 1995, after 25 million years of domination and conquest.

4.) Alpha Aries: (Hamal)
Alpha Aries (Hamal), as another marvelous life supporting solar system was first colonized by Galactic Federation human colonists from Andromeda and Lyra, about 2.5 million years ago. The third planet from the Alpha Aries star is a bit smaller than Earth, and is occupied by the present offshoots of those human colonists described above. It is a beautiful water planet like Earth, containing only three large continents, and also like Earth, it is hollow. The human residents (numbering 700 million) all live in crystal cities scattered throughout its interior.

The fourth and fifth planets, as we go outward from Alpha Aries, are each about 7,400 miles in diameter. They are both more semi-arid worlds, and are occupied by a hybrid human / dinosaurian species that are peacefully co-existing with those folks on the third planet, as previously described. The drier climate of these two particular planets is more suitable for comfortable living, to those people in particular, much as it would also have been for a pure reptilian species.

The Dinosaurians from Orion, about 2 million years ago, had captured a defense colony of Andromedans in the Alpha Aries system, and created a hybrid race of Dinosaurian/ Humans by means of successful genetic alteration. (Their scientists then, were a great deal more advanced than any of ours are at our present moment in time, with no guesswork...) Those successfully hybridized folks are the people who now occupy the drier fourth and fifth planets in the Alpha Aries solar system.

The original humans on the third planet are mostly the same as those folks that have been described earlier, in other solar systems, who had originally immigrated from the Lyra and Sirius B human sources, with probably only minor differences.

5.) Eta Hercules:
The constellation of Hercules is one of the five largest in our night sky, and a major summer star-group in our northern hemisphere. It is situated between the constellations of Draco (Greek for Dragon), and Ophiuchus (Greek for Serpent Bearer). Eta Hercules, like Alpha Aries, was originally colonized, about 2.5 million years ago, when the Galactic Federation was setting up their series of strategically located defense colonies, and joined the Galactic Federation of Light about 2.4 million years ago.

The entire constellation of Draco is occupied by reptilians, and Ophiuchus, which now also has human civilizations, was originally exclusively occupied by reptilians at that time, as well. An Eta Hercules defense colony, for protection against predatory reptilians, was a logical and practical idea when it was first settled by humans.

It should be said here, that most life supporting planets, of the millions of those in this galaxy, do have a serious diversity of mammals, amphibians, reptilians, sea creatures and plants. Just like there are very intelligent ensouled humans living on this planet, and there are also monkeys and apes here, we should not assume that just because a solar system or planet thereof is not controlled by reptilians, that it does not have a diversity of reptilian species. Most of them do.

The Eta Hercules solar system consists of 6 planets, and its humans occupy the third planet outward from Eta Hercules. Its first planet is too close to its sun, and not amenable to life. Its second planet has a rather hot environment, and in spite of that it supports a very diverse ecosystem, with fish, reptilians, amphibians, birds, bats, etc., and a great diversity of plant life. It is bit too warm for full time comfortable occupation by the humans from the third planet.

The Eta Hercules people treat this semi-arid world as an elaborate, on-going study in biological diversity by their life scientists. The remaining planets in the Eta Hercules solar system are gas giants, similar in many ways to our Jupiter, Saturn, Uranus or Neptune. As a closing comment, I should mention here, that Eta Hercules is about 112 light years from Earth.

6.) Eta Pegasus:
Eta Pegasus is Located in the constellation of Pegasus, also referred to as the Pegasus Star League. The Constellation of Pegasus is an immense cluster of more than 1000 stars, which ranges from 35 to 400 light years from Earth. The Pegasus Star League consists of hundreds of member solar systems. We should bear in mind, that more often than not, there is more than one fully occupied planet in each solar system. We are speaking of a humongous number of individual human populated planets in the Pegasus Star League.

When human kind, speaking of our own direct ancestors in this galaxy, evolved as a fully sentient species in the constellation of Vega, they soon began to explore across this part of the galaxy. It appears that their first two main colonial groups were started in the Sirius B system, and the Constellation of Pegasus. The Pegasus star League is one of the older members of the Galactic Federation, becoming a member as early as 3.78 million years ago. The constellation of Pegasus is positioned between the constellations of Cygnus (Swan), and Aquarius (Water Carrier), in the winter and autumn skies of the northern hemisphere.

Three major species of human co-exist in the Pegasian Star League. The first is much like the Sirian human in height and appearance, and is divided into the same white and blue skin types. The second is a thinner human whose skin is red or orange. The third species is a hybrid of the Dinosaurian and the second humanoid.

7.) The Pleiades: (In the Constellation of Taurus)
The Pleiades are recognized and referred to as the "seven sisters", with reference to the 7 brightest stars in the Pleiadean star cluster, as seen from Earth. Our sun has erroneously been referred to as the 8th. Star in the Pleiadean star cluster, but is really not that in the Pleiadean system of things. Our sun is in orbit around Alcyone, one of the seven sisters. The Pleiades is an immense star cluster, of more than 2,500 stars, in the Constellation of Taurus. Our position at its outer fringe would seem rather insignificant, although it might be affording us a clearer view of our neighboring constellations.

Two hundred planetary systems of the Pleiadean star cluster have united to form the Pleiadean Star League. There are obviously many others out there who have decided not to join anything, as would happen with our own human types.

The ancestors of the Pleiadean Star League originated in the Constellations of Andromeda and Lyra, and settled in the Pleiades about 400,000 years ago. The Pleiadean Star League joined the Galactic Federation about 300,000 years ago.

Pleiadeans resemble Earth humans. The first type is a Caucasian, with features varying from the so-called "Nordic", with blonde hair, blue eyes and pale skin, to a Mediterranean type, with dark to light brown hair, gray to brown eyes, and tanned looking skin. The second type looks typically Asian, with dark hair, dark almond shaped eyes, and skin that can vary from very pale to dark brown.

The eyes of all Pleiadeans are slightly larger than those of Earth humans. Their thin lips are very pale pink, while their ears are fitted slightly lower on the side of the head and are somewhat smaller in size. Their hands and feet are delicate in appearance, with long fingers and toes. Men vary from 5 feet 10 inches to almost 7 feet in height, and women vary from 5 feet 7 inches to almost 6 feet 4 inches in height. Pleiadeans require only about 2 hours of sleep per day.

Pleiadean languages vary from a dialect similar to German or Swiss German to a smoother and more lyrical variant spoken mostly in star nations located in and around the star Maia. Largely, we could look upon the Pleiadeans as our closest genetic relatives. However, the human race at large as it exists on this planet is said to be based on something like 46 variants of our own particular species in this galaxy, with each varying to a small extent from each of the others.

8.) Sirius B: (The Sirius B solar system in the Constellation of Canis Major)

I remember Sirius (Sirius B) being referred to as the "Dog Star" when I was a high school student. Canis Major = great dog, in Latin. A long time ago, I learned that the African tribe, called the "Dogons" referred to Sirius B as being where they came from.

Originally, the solar system of the star Sirius A had been settled about 6 million years ago, by a sentient species of Lions called the "Paschat", meaning "Warriors of Heaven". When settlers from the Constellation of Lyra arrived, they appealed to the Paschat, and to the local galactic and spiritual Hierarchies. With their combined approval, the Lyran settlers established their initial settlements in the Sirius B solar system, and later, in the Sirius C and D solar systems.

Sirius B is situated about 8.3 light years from Earth. The third planet, with two moons was settled over four million years ago. It is called "Atarmunk" = holy place of the Atar. The atar is a golden eagle type of bird, six feet tall, which is celebrated for its valor, wisdom and loyalty to its mate. This particular planet is occupied by more than 600 million people. The fourth planet, called "Muktarin" is also completely occupied by humans and is headquarters for the Sirius B Galactic Federation mission, including diplomatic liaison and defense operations.

The typical humans of Sirius B, C and D have been much earlier described as having its men with either perfectly formed, muscular physiques, to child like figures and they vary from 6 feet 6 inches to 7 feet 4 inches tall. Women are extremely voluptuous and stand between 6 feet 2 inches and 6 feet 8 inches tall. Sirian hair is blonde or light brown, and their skin in tones is extremely pale, light red or light blue. Eyes are light blue to green.

B.)   Cetacians:

Nu Ceti - In the Constellation of Cetus (The Whale)
Nu Ceti is described as a distant earth-like white / yellow sun, and is positioned in the Constellation of Cetus. She is approximately 810 light years from Earth. Nu Ceti is situated in the Northern Hemisphere, between the Constellations of Aries, Pisces and Eridanus, in the southern part of our autumn and winter skies.

The fascinating people of Nu Ceti were once considered the greatest traders in the galaxy. They had originally become members of the Galactic Federation about 2.5 million years ago. However, Nu Ceti withdrew from its Federation membership, to resume its previously neutral status, about 5000 years ago.

The main reason for this was that neutrality was a safer

position for them than Federation membership, particularly as the reptilians in their more recent attacks were coming closer to Nu Ceti. Also, at the time of their declaration of neutrality, they stopped anyone from coming too close to their solar system, and also ceased their trading activities which normally extended far across the galaxy.

The Nu Cetians are primarily agricultural people, so their main items of trade related back to agriculture as a rule. They used to trade with us until they went neutral 5000 years ago, and much of this activity took place in China. They are responsible for bringing us citrus fruit, onions, garlic, and other tuber plants like potatoes. Their one exception in trade with us was that they brought us our domestic cats.

These neat little folks are land cetaceans that look like small short tailed bears. They are covered with multihued brown fur that varies in color from dark chocolate to very light tan. Nu Cetian society is matriarchal, where descendants are traced back through their mothers.

Although its head is shaped like a bear's, it has a large snout like mouth, and very powerful jaws. Its large prominent black eyes are very light sensitive, indicative of its former nocturnal life style. With human type ears located on the sides of the head, its sense of hearing is acute.

The Nu Cetian is a biped, with a highly developed sense of gravity. Its two muscular arms end in paw like hands that contain 4 stubby fingers each. Its legs are very muscular, and it has 2 long wide feet that each end in 3 stubby clawed toes. Their language is similar to Chinese with some added differences. The Nu Cetians are very scientifically advanced and had long ago created much of the finest cloaking technology in the galaxy. The reptilians wanted it, and actually attacked the Nu Cetians, devastating their home planet, in an attempt to steal the technology.

C.) Equians:

Arcturus (Alpha Bootes) - In the Constellation of Bootes:
Arcturus is about 37 light years from Earth. It is the brightest star (a glittering orange giant) in the Constellation of Bootes. It is located between Ursa Major (Big Bear), and Virgo (Maiden).

The Arcturus Confederation sits on the same Federation regional council which will soon become our own future district assembly. Arcturus has an 8 planet system, with its third and fourth planets both occupied by its equian citizens.

The Arcturians are this galaxy's greatest healers, and they look upon this type of service to others as their most important contribution to all other societies.

Arcturians are a highly sentient mammalian species that looks somewhat like a horse. They are bipeds however, and have a rather tall slender body with a somewhat stylized horse's head. Arcturian skin color ranges from a vanilla shade to a very dark brown. A mane grows on the back of the neck and head, and they have a very thin tail that only slightly resembles that of a horse. The arms legs and body seem very muscular, and their hands end in fingers that are very long, supple and rather thin. Arcturian eyes are much larger than those of humans and are either pale blue or dark brown in color. Their ears correspond to those of a horse, but are smaller and more rounded than those of our Earth horses.

The Arcturians at the present time are contributing much toward the assimilation by the Federation of the reptilian star nation groups. They are trusted and respected by the reptilians, and virtually every other species in the galaxy.

D.) - Reptilians - Including Dinosaurians:

Before moving on with general descriptions and details

concerning the reptilians, even though there have been earlier comments on the subject, I will now proceed, with a very brief outline of their history, Sheldan Nidle, in his marvelous book, "Your Galactic Neighbors" provided an outline of the earlier history of the reptilians and their vast empires which had evolved over a very long period of time.

Most of us Earth humans have a close to zero knowledge of extraterrestrials of any kind. We could not even imagine that reptilians were already active and evolving at a very fast rate in this galaxy for more than 25 million years before we turned up on the scene. The reptilians were chosen by the dark side of our reality to become the great conquerors and the negative side of things within our universe of duality. Duality means good and bad.

Things like conflict, constant lies and untruth, domination, lack of sustenance, and enslavement relate to the dark side. Of course, on the light side, or the good side, we would find the opposites. If we are looking for those opposites here, at the moment of this writing, it is obvious that the dark side is running things on this planet Earth.

Way back about 35 million years ago, the negative God we refer to as Satan, in a female embodiment, and referred to as "Anchara", made the choice, mentioned above. Great reptilian hatcheries were set up on certain planets in the Sagittarius Constellation. Ten million years later, in the process of upward evolution, the then very sentient and highly intelligent reptilians already had spacecraft and were beginning to roam the galaxy on the path of conquest. (They had been told by their God, Anchara, that only they, the reptilians, were the chosen race of sentient beings in this galaxy, and that they were free to go out there and conquer and subjugate or destroy any other sentient species, as they might choose.)

In any event, in speaking of this entire galaxy, we are dealing with almost countless numbers of planets occupied by highly sentient species, with many of those species being capable of space travel, and a great deal more than just that. When we speak of humans eventually being able to match or move technologically beyond the reptilians, there was a very basic reason for that, in spite of the exceptional intelligence of the reptilians. Those of the light, or the positive side, have the clear and ready potential when they are born, to be or to become highly creative in their thinking.

The dark or negative side can intimidate, harass and conquer many of those on the side of the light, but they are not creative, and if they need newer or better ideas, they have to get them from the light side, by whatever means, including stealing. The usual way those folks dealt with that, is that once the group or civilization with the desired technology was conquered, who owned what was a moot point, as the conqueror obviously could take it all.

There were no highly sentient, or technologically advanced reptilians in the Constellation of Orion to begin with. They migrated to Orion, mostly from the Constellation of Draco. This involved setting up main bases of operation toward conquering this portion of the galaxy. The native reptilian species in the Constellation of Orion were still crawling on the ground at that time.

1.) Bellatrix: - (Gamma Orion) - In the Constellation of Orion
The Constellation of Orion is a distant group of larger magnitude stars and star clusters in the night sky.

It is positioned between the constellations of Taurus and Canis Major, and just below the constellation of Auriga. There are three very bright stars located at the center of the constellation of Orion. Just to the right and slightly above Orion's belt there is a bright blue star, and that is Bellatrix.

Bellatrix is approximately 245 light years from Earth. Its solar system has 8 planets, with its third and fourth planets being occupied by the reptilians. The third planet, a highly oxygenated water world is 11,000 miles in diameter, and serves as their home world. The fourth planet, about 15,000 miles in diameter, and semi-arid, has many sacred sites where the reptilians honor their solar system and beautiful planets.

The predominant species inhabiting Bellatrix is a Dinosaurian / Reptilian hybrid that first migrated from the Constellation of Draco about 25 million years ago. The body is typically very scaly and bony. The upper head is surrounded by a large bony crest, and the eyes are large and set forward just above and to either side of a very small nose. The mouth is distinguished by thin lips that extend from one side of the head to the other.

The ears are non-existent, with their only indication being an extra smooth 3 inch circle on either side of the head, just behind the eyes. The eyes are large, red or dull yellow and resemble those of Earth's reptiles. The skin has a crocodile's scaliness and can be green, yellow, brown or red. A small bony crest that runs up the middle of the back is connected to the larger crest at the top of the head.

The being is a biped. It has thin hands with six long, clawed fingers, and feet that have five toes ending in stubby razor sharp claws.

Its tail, which is very short and thick like a crocodile's reaches only as far as its feet. As with most of the reptilians, the male is shorter than the female. Males are 8 to 10 feet tall, and females are 8.5 to 10.25 feet tall.

2.) Eta Draconis: - in the Constellation of Draco (Draco = Dragon)
Eta Draconis is about 88 light years from Earth. It is a giant yellow star located between the constellations of Ursa Major (Big Bear), and Ursa Minor (Little Bear), which contains the Big and Little Dipper respectively. Eta Draconis has an 8 planet solar system, and its third and fourth planets are

occupied by the reptilians. Those planets have a generally drier desert type of climate, which is more ideal for reptilians.

The Eta Draconian rulers were their empire's diplomats and overseers, and Eta Draconis was the main headquarters for their diplomatic corps, which was spread throughout the Anchara Alliance. Prior to the treaty as recently (1994-95) completed between the Anchara Alliance and the Galactic Federation, there were large reptilian empires in Sagittarius, Draco and Orion, which were most directly related to reptilian activities in the entire galaxy. Other smaller and more scattered groups also existed in our general region, but have been far less aggressive or wanting to be dominant over humans, cetaceans and amphibians.

It is important to note here that once the Treaty of Anchara was completed, the Eta Draconian rulers realized they had a duty to ensure that this peace process could be achieved. They then took it upon themselves to see to it that the other nations in the Draconian Empire and the Anchara Alliance would agree to have their regional councils join the Galactic Federation.

The reptilians in the Eta Draconis solar system are a Dinosaurian / reptilian shape shifter hybrid that migrated from the Constellation of Cepheus approximately 35 million years ago. Typically, their bodies are very scaly with occasional prominent ridges and crests. The top of the head is crowned by a large crest that rims the forehead and stretches down the back. Large eyes are set on either side of a very small nose. They are either brown or dull yellow, and resemble those of Earth's snakes. Thin dark lips extend from one side of the head to the other. The ears are large circular membranes more than 7 inches in diameter, located on either side of the head, just behind the eyes.

The skin has the rough scaliness of a reptile, and glistens like that of a crocodile, alligator or toad, and is green, yellow, brown or red. A narrow ridge running up the middle of the back is connected to the larger ridge on the back of the head. The being is biped, and has thin hands with three long clawed fingers and four toed feet that have short, very sharp claws.

The tail is very large and narrow, like a reptile's and extends just beyond the feet. Males stand 7.5 to 8 feet tall, and females typically taller, stand between 8.25 and 9.5 feet tall.

3.) <u>Sigma Draconis:</u> - This is another solar system close to Eta Draconis.
Sigma Draconis is a type K orange star, in the Constellation of Draco, and is about 18.8 light years from Earth.

The reptilian Star-Nation of Sigma Draconis is brought forth as an example here, as it has been the most significant warrior nation of them all. The Sigma Draconians long ago became the pre-eminent officer corps of the Draconian Empire. Their skill, courage and strategies in battle, coupled with having the most advanced weaponry, led the Sigma Draconians to become the most feared star nation in the Anchara Alliance.

When the Treaty of Anchara was completed, the Sigma Draconians, being the most powerful military leaders in the Alliance, took it upon themselves, much the same as the Eta Draconians had just done, to assure that the path to peace was honorably observed. The Sigma Draconians even organized successful campaigns to cut short any Alliance rebellion against peace.

Sigma Draconis has a 12 planet solar system. Its first two planets are too hot and not amenable to normal life, and the third has a corrosive atmosphere like Venus, after having been exploited by the rulers of Sigma Draconis as a testing site for weapons for use in galactic wars.

The fourth and fifth planets are occupied by the Sigma Draconians. The fourth planet, 10,000 miles in diameter, is surrounded by an atmosphere similar to our own, but typical of a reptilian occupied planet it is a drier planet than Earth. The fifth planet slightly larger, is a true water world which has 7 continents, with three of them quite dry, and more comfortable for reptilians. The six remaining planets in the system are gas giants much like the ones in our own solar system.

The reptilians on Sigma Draconis are dragon-like, and first migrated from the Constellation of Sagittarius approximately 25 million years ago. The Sigma Draconians closely resemble dragons and typify the conventional Earth concept of demons. They are characterized by extreme scaliness and for us, are frightful to look at.

Like Earth's reptiles, the large red or yellow eyes of the Sigma Draconians are set forward just above and to either side of a very narrow snout. Its mouth consists of thin lips that extend from one side of the head to the other.

The teeth are large, and clearly those of a predator, while the ears are small and scaly. The skin has the scaliness of a crocodile, and is yellow, green, brown or red. The body is long and lanky, with a scaly crest extending down the back. There is a small set of bat-like wings on the back.

The being is a biped, with thin hands ending in six long clawed fingers, and its feet have five toes tipped with small razor sharp claws. An arrow-like point marks the end of the long thin tail, and its body and breath wreak of brimstone.

Why were our great artists and sculptors so capable, hundreds of years ago, of completely illustrating and sculpting such a scary being?

I find it bothersome, that our historically held concept of dragons and demons should be so completely personified by this particular being. Nothing we could find in the way of published material has ever suggested, or related back to these particular reptilians. Draco means Dragon, so there surely is a connection.

Our world has been quietly directed and governed by privileged families and secret societies, extending downward from the Illuminati, who are basically at the top, and have themselves been governed by reptilians until 1994. These societies with their quiet strangle hold on all levels of government, the courts, publishers, education and at the top, the entire money system, have been very successful in hiding anything they don't want us to know.

As stated earlier, there are thousands of planets out there which are occupied by reptilians, all the way from Sagittarius, to Draco, to Orion, with numerous other smaller areas where only a small part of a constellation is occupied by reptilians. Now that the reptilian groups of planets have virtually all joined the Galactic Federation since 1995-96, they are to be looked upon by us as our friends. They are eager to provide us with technology and help us clean up our planet, toward making amends for having been our predatory enemies for millions of years.

Later on in this book, we will again refer to the Annunaki, a race of hybrid reptilians, who were members of the Anchara Alliance, and who, through the Illuminati, had controlled us for many millennia. Farther behind the scenes, the Annunaki were also controlled by the Anchara Alliance Empire, headquartered in the Bellatrix solar system. The big surprise about to be revealed to us ignorant Earth humans in the rather near future, is that away back, since the time of Atlantis, this planet has had a reptilian form of government. We describe that situation somewhat, later on, after covering the other examples of sentient races and species out there. A simple comparison of an Anchara Alliance society to a Galactic Federation society is provided in the descriptive information provided in our discussion of the star nation of Rigel.

Here we go again, with the diversity of highly intelligent,

sentient beings in this galaxy, who are beyond us in development, and capable of traveling throughout the galaxy by their own means as developed by themselves. The Amphibians are next, and they are also a very intelligent and capable species . . .

E.) The Amphibians:

1.) The Star Nation of Mintaka (Delta Orionis) - in the Constellation of Orion
Mintaka is actually what our astronomers refer to as Mintaka C. It is one of the companion stars encircling the prime star, Delta Orionis-A. This is a 6 planet solar system, where its third planet is the only one occupied by the highly intelligent species of amphibians we will be describing here.

It is a semi-tropical water planet, where one of her continents in particular, is noted for its vast swamps, surrounded by slightly higher ground, covered with lush grasses. It would appear that this set the stage for the more complete development of the Mintakans, our amphibian neighbors. On a drier continent on this magnificent water world, a smaller population of dinosaurian-reptilians have their civilization. They get along fine with the amphibians, as they have co-existed for millions of years in close proximity to each other.

About 30 million years ago Mintaka's amphibians created a new civilization which became a major star nation in this sector of this galaxy. About 25 million years ago, Mintaka's nation of amphibians was conquered and taken over by reptilian forces of the Draconian Empire. Mintaka had remained part of the Anchara Alliance ever since that time, until 1996, when, like most other member states and groups of the Anchara Alliance, Mintaka joined the Galactic Federation.

The Mintakan amphibian majority co-exists with a minority of reptilian and dinosaurian hybrids. In many ways the Mintakan amphibian species resembles our frogs and toads, but there are significant differences. They are bipeds. Their skin, which is smooth and hairless, is typically iridescent, in colors ranging from bright red, orange and green to yellow and brown. Mintakan eyes, unlike those of Earth's amphibians, protrude only slightly. They are large, bright red, orange or greenish yellow in color, and extend a bit around the side of the head. The large head seems disproportionate to the rest of the body, and the short neck seems almost non-existent. The body, arms and legs are very muscular. Each limb has four long thin webbed digits, and the toes end in small claws.

Mintakan males are 7 to 8 feet in height, and the females are between 7.5 and 8.5 feet tall. The species is also characterized by three small ridges which extend the length of the back, and end up at the top of the head.

2.) Beta Canceri (Al Tarf) - in the Constellation of Cancer.
The constellation of Cancer, positioned in the winter skies of the northern hemisphere, is surrounded by the constellations of Gemini, Leo, Canis Major, and Hydra. Al Tarf is Cancer's brightest star, and is located about 290 light years from Earth.

Al Tarf had been part of a series of star nations captured 8 million years ago by the Draconian Empire. She succeeded in freeing herself from the Draconian Empire about 4 million years ago, and at that time, joined the Galactic Federation. The Al Tarf solar system consists of six planets, and the third planet, a large water world nearly 17,000 miles in diameter, is occupied by the amphibian population. The Al Tarfans are very similar to the amphibian citizens of Mintaka, in the constellation of Orion, so no separate details will be provided here.

The Al Tarfans have tremendous psychic abilities, and are skilled at manipulating the minds of others. They have amassed massive libraries of scientific and spiritual knowledge, dating back more than 18 million years.

3.) Rigel (Beta Orionis) - in the Constellation of Orion.

Since they are more closely related to their amphibian, rather than dinosaurian heritage, they are included in this section dealing with amphibians. You might note, interestingly, that as an amphibian hybrid, the Rigelians were capable enough to end up controlling a lot of the reptilian empire. Rigel became the military headquarters for this sector of the Anchara Alliance, and chief builder and supplier of armed spacecraft and other armaments to the rest of the Alliance, and had remained in that position, until they joined the Galactic Federation, in 1997.

The Rigel solar system contains 12 planets. The first two are very hot and not very supportive of life. The third, about the size of Venus, has a similar hot surface, with an atmosphere of gases which are not life supporting. This condition was caused by the Rigelians, who used that planet for conducting experiments with advanced space weaponry. (It is said that the reptilians did roughly the same things to Venus and Mars about 1 million years ago.) The fourth planet in the Rigel solar system is a semi-arid planet, much larger than earth, and has been set up with many battle ground sequences for the training of reptilian military forces. The fifth, a bit more than 11,000 miles in diameter, is a true water world. and serves as the Rigelian home world. It has 7 continents, with 2 being very dry, and the other 5, having inland seas, and is lush with vegetation.

The Rigelians, like virtually all of the other reptilian based nations are now busily changing their society from a hierarchical model, to one in which the lower castes, once treated like slaves, are given a greater voice in their society's decision making process. They are now rapidly moving toward the Galactic Federation model of society which recognizes the needs, creativity and highest potential of every person in their society.

The predominant species in the Rigel star system is a dinosaurian / amphibian (shape shifter) hybrid that migrated

115

from the constellation of Cancer about 15 million years ago. The body has extreme scaliness, with a scattering of prominent ridges. A wide crest surrounds the skull at forehead level and runs down the back of the head to the neck, where it connects to a narrow ridge that extends down the middle of the back. The eyes, average in size, are set on either side of a very small nose. The mouth is edged in thin dark lips that stretch from one side of the head to the other. An unusually smooth hollow, about 5 inches in diameter on either side of the head represents the otherwise non-existent ears. Rigelian eyes are brown or dull yellow, and resemble those of Earth's reptilians. Their skin which is green, yellow, brown or red has both dinosaurian scaliness and the smooth shine of an amphibian. The male ranges from 7 to 8.5 feet tall, and the female ranges from 8 to 9.25 feet tall. They require 4 to 5 hours of sleep per day,

F.) Mixed Species:

1.) The Star Nation of Aldebaran (Alpha Tauri)
Situated Northwest of Orion, between Auriga and Gemini, Aldebaran is a bright orange star, directly in front of, and below the Pleiades star cluster. The Aldebaran solar system consists of 8 planets, with its second planet occupied by reptilians and its fourth occupied by hybrid humans, who look much like Earth humans. They were crossed with reptilians, and the Draconian Empire terra formed their planet to become a proper home for them, more than 2 million years ago. Aldebaran finally managed, about 800,000 years ago, to break away from the Anchara Alliance, and joined the Galactic Federation.

The reptilian is lizard-like, very scaly and muscular. The skin is multi-colored in green and blue or red and green mixed with yellow, black or purple. The eyes are large and round, with reptile like vertical slits of sky blue, red or gold. The hands, narrower than those of a human, consist of four digits that end in a short sharp claw. The feet have five long toes, which end in short curved claws. The tail is small and bulbous.

The female, slightly taller than the male has a height of just less than 7 feet.

The human hybrid from Aldebaran has a vague resemblance to Earth humans. The male is slight in build with a well-proportioned body, head and limbs, and stands between 6 and 7.25 feet tall. Females are strong and symmetrical, with a height varying from 5 feet 8 inches to 6 feet 7 inches. Large round or almond shaped eyes are brown, black, blue, green or hazel. Hair is blonde, brown, black or red. Both species, reptilians and humans need only 2 to 4 hours sleep per day. Earlier in their history, Aldebarans' were the master diplomats in the Draconian Empire.

2.) The Great Star Union of Centaurus
We will look at two of their home worlds, with one at 4.39 light years away, and the second, at about 410 light years away. The constellation of Centaurus is very large, with its farthest away home world being about 1000 light years away from Earth.

This Galaxy is a very big place!!!

Alpha Centauri (Rigel Centaurus) - This is one of the 3 stars of a "triple star" referred to by our astronomers as Proxima Centauri.
Alpha Centauri is 4.39 light years away from Earth, and as such, is also probably the one closest planet to Earth that is occupied by an intelligent space-faring species. The Alpha Centaurians joined the Galactic Federation 1.1 million years ago. Alpha Centauri Was originally colonized by humans from Lyra a little less than 2.5 million years ago, and contains one of the larger Centaurus water worlds, which they refer to as "Endo". Endo has immense oceans, teeming with life, and her beautiful sky dazzles with nightglow. The nightglow is caused by the outermost layer of her 3 - layer firmament, which becomes electrified from the coronal discharges from her sun. They fill the night sky with a soft pastel glow that

covers every color of the spectrum, particularly blues, greens and violets. In her seas are whales larger than those of Earth.

It is of further interest to note here that Atlantean leaders fled to the Alpha Centauri planetary system for refuge, as soon as our flood began here on Earth.

Lamda Centauri

This is the Solar system as mentioned above, which is 410 light years away from Earth, and it contains two large water worlds. Lamda Centauri's third planet was first colonized nearly 1.3 million years ago, by people from Andromeda and Eridanus. A second group of colonists settled a neighboring water world, four times larger, and this world was even more astounding than the first. Her atmosphere glowed with a brightness that filled this world with irrepressible energies. The singing and glowing atmosphere of this magnificent world produced wondrous healing energy that energized all people exposed to it.

Human Centaurans closely resemble Earth humans. The male is very muscular and well proportioned, and ranges from 6 to 8 feet tall. The female, also well formed, but less muscular, ranges from 5 feet 5 inches to 7 feet tall. Centaurian hair is blonde, brown, black or red. Skin color is either very dark brown or tan. Eyes, either almond shaped or round are brown, black blue, green or hazel.

There is no reference in the main source of this material by Sheldan Nidle, that the Centaurian reptile species came from anywhere else. Those particular reptilians are really quite unique.

The body of the reptilian Centaurian is very lizardly and muscular, with variegated skin of either blue and green or red and green. The eyes are round and bulging, with reptile-like vertical slits in either bright red or gold. The hands are narrower than those of a human and each has 6 digits, which end in razor sharp curved claws. The feet have long toes ending in the same curved claw as the hands. There is no tail. The female is just less than 8 feet tall, and that is slightly taller than the male, and interestingly enough, this reptilian Centaurian requires only 2 to 4 hours of sleep per day, so they match the best case for humans.

3.) The Star Nation of Sabik - In the Constellation of Ophiuchus (Greek = "Serpent Bearer")

This star nation is about 84 light years from Earth, it is a major summer star group in the night skies of our Northern Hemisphere. It is located between the constellations of Hercules, Scorpius and Serpens.

Originally a society of neutral reptilians, the Sabik people approached the Galactic Federation nearly 2.8 million years ago, and asked the Federation to establish a human defense colony on their star nation. Human colonists were sent there from the Andromedan Confederacy, as well as from various other star nations in the constellation of Lyra. The people of Sabik have been Federation members since that time.

Sabik is an 8 planet solar system. Its fourth planet is a swampy water planet, 8,500 miles in diameter, with 6 seas and 4 continents. It is the home of the reptilians. Its fifth planet, close to the same size is a semi-tropical water world with 7 continents, and is not as marshy as the previous planet. This planet is occupied by Sabik's human population. The major export of the peoples of Sabik to the rest of the Galaxy is their talent of explaining to others how easily reptilians and humans can co-exist. The body of the reptilian is very lizardly and muscular, and bears a close resemblance to the many reptilian species in the constellation of Orion. With a height of just under 8 feet, the female is taller than the male. Their skin is scaly with patches of blue and green or red and green. Its hands, narrower than those of a human, have 6 digits ending in a sharp claw. The feet, with 5 long toes have the same curved claw. Eyes are round and bulging, with reptile-like vertical slits of bright red or gold. The tail is short and slender. These folks need about 4 hours of sleep per day.

The Sabik human resembles the present day Earth human. The male is powerfully built and well proportioned. The female is shapely but less muscular. Males range from just under 6 feet to 8 feet in height. Females range from 5 feet 5 inches to 7 feet 6 inches in height. Their skin is either very dark brown or slightly tanned, while hair is blonde, brown, black or red. Round or almond shaped eyes can be brown, black, blue, green or hazel. These folks need only about two hours of sleep per day.

4.) The Star Nation of Tau Ceti - In the Constellation of Cetus.
This star nation is 11.8 light years from Earth. The Tau Ceti solar system has 12 planets. There are two main home worlds. The first, being its third planet, is a lush forest planet, and a true water world. It is 8,500 miles in diameter. This home world is occupied by a race of land cetaceans, who look somewhat like Earth's large Grizzly bears, with some important differences.

The second home world is somewhat larger than the first, and is a true water world with 7 continents. It was settled, as a human defense colony by people from the constellation of Hercules, at the request of the cetaceans, about 2.4 million years ago. The cetaceans had already joined the Federation about 2.5 million years ago. The humans of Tau Ceti closely resemble the humans of the constellation of Hercules. There are three predominant skin colors, being brown, reddish brown and dark and light shades of red and green.

The cetaceans are huge furry beings with bear-like bodies covered in brown, black or light golden brown fur and they have small furry tails. Their heads are shaped like those of bears, but with smaller muzzles, the teeth look more like those of a human than a bear. The eyes, set forward on the head, similar to those of a human, are brown, blue or black. The ears, which resemble those of Earth's bears, are positioned just above the eyes at the sides of the head. They are bipeds, and have a higher center of gravity than the bears of Earth. Their two muscular arms have paw-like hands and 5 five stubby, clawed fingers. Very muscular legs end in comparatively small feet with 5 short thick toes each. These bear-like beings range from 9 to 12 feet in height.

The inhabitants of Tau Ceti are celebrated for their expertise in designing some of the most advanced ships in the Galactic Federation's exploration fleets. They are also considered some of the best pilots and navigators in the galaxy.

5.) The Star Nation of Procyon - in the Constellation of Canis Minor.
This star nation is located approximately 11.4 light years from Earth. Procyon is a binary star. Her solar system, Procyon A, consists of 6 planets. Its third and fourth planets are both water worlds, and each is about 9,800 miles in diameter. Its third planet is occupied by its amphibian / reptilian people. Its fourth planet is occupied by humans, originally from Sirius B, who arrived there about 3.9 million years ago.

At the same time, reptilian refugees from the constellation of cancer arrived there as well, and each group chose the planet most suitable for them, where the fourth planet, occupied by the reptilians is a drier world than the fifth planet, occupied by the humans.

The humans are a pure Lyran / Sirian human, like those on Sirius B. They are either blue or white skinned, and look much like the humans on Earth, with two major differences. First, their eyes which range in shades of blue green and brown are much larger and more alert, while their two ears, smaller than ours, are joined to the head at a lower level. Second, the top and back of the head is enlarged to accommodate a larger brain capacity. Males are 6 feet 6 inches to 7 feet 4 inches tall, and females are 6 feet 4 inches to 7 feet tall. These folks need only one to two hours of sleep per day.

The reptilians possess lizard-like bodies covered with scaly skin. Their head is almost round, and in proportion to the rest of the body, while the neck is short and well defined. Wide set bulging brown or red eyes are placed on either side of a very thin ridged nose that ends in two slit-like nostrils. The eyes move independently of each other. Their ears are small 2 inch ovals set just behind each eye. The mouth is a thin lipped slit extending from ear to ear. The body and appendages of this being are very muscular. It has 4 thin nail-less fingers, and three long sharply clawed toes. Its stunted tail looks like a small hump at the base of the spine. Typical of a reptilian, the females are a bit larger than the males, and range from 7 to 8 feet tall. The males range from 7 feet to 7 feet 8 inches tall. These amphibian / reptilians only require 3 to 4 hours of sleep per day. The beings of Procyon are known as gifted scientists and avid explorers.

6.) The Confederation of Fomalhaut (Alpha Pisces Austrini) - in the Constellation of Pisces.
Fomalhaut, a blazing white star, is located in the Southern Hemisphere, immediately beneath and between Aquarius and Capricorn, and is about 25 light years from Earth.

It is an 8 planet solar system. It was first colonized by a gang of human rebels from the Pleiades, about 250,000 years ago, and then, about 50,000 years later, a smaller band of dinosaurian / reptilians from Bellatrix in Orion, arrived. There were intermittent wars between these two groups until they finally came to terms and signed a mutual peace agreement, about 20,000 years ago.

The third planet, 9,000 miles in diameter, is a large water world which was first colonized by the Pleiadean rebels. The fourth planet, 8,000 miles in diameter is also occupied by the former Pleiadeans.

The fifth planet, approximately 15,000 miles in diameter, is a semi-arid planet, and is occupied by the amphibian / reptilians.

Fomalhaut humans are of two distinct body types. The first closely resembles the so-called Nordic type, and is usually blonde with bright blue or steel-gray eyes. Men of this type are muscular and stand approximately six feet tall. Their women are well-favored and range from about 5 feet 6 inches to slightly under 6 feet tall. The second type has darker, almost tanned looking skin and dark brown hair with brown, grey or black eyes. They have the same relative height and appearance as the first mentioned Nordic group. Both types require 2 to 4 hours of sleep per day.

The dinosaurian / reptilians of Fomalhaut are hybrids who originated from the star Bellatrix in Orion. Typically, they are very scaly and bony. The upper head is surrounded by a large bony crest and the eyes are large and set forward just above and to either side of a very small nose. The mouth has thin lips that extend from one side of the head to the other. The non-existent ears are represented by an extra smooth 3 inch circle on either side of the head, and just behind the eyes. Large eyes, resembling those of Earth's reptiles, are either red or dull yellow. The skin is scaly, like that of a crocodile, and can be green, yellow, brown or red. A small bony crest stretches up the middle of the back and connects to a larger crest on the crown of the head. The being is a biped. Its hands are thin with 6 long clawed fingers. Its feet have 5 toes that each end in a small, knifelike claw. The tail is very short and thick like a crocodile's and reaches only to the feet. Males range from 8 to 10 feet tall, and females are 6 inches taller at both ends of the scale. These beings require 4 to 6 hours of sleep per day.

By merging the best points of galactic human society to those of the clan-like dinosaurian / reptilian one, the Fomalhautans have created a culture that works. They are now able to demonstrate and explain some of the obvious differences which are likely to be experienced with first contact, where the Federation is about to set up first contact with a new or soon to become member nation. Earth is the example that we are looking at, not long from this point in time in the year 2008.

General Comments Concerning the Solar Systems We Have Covered:

Most of the odd creatures that have existed in the geological history of our planet are presently in existence in a similar form on one or more of the planets we have covered. Such would include Terradactyls, and similar reptilian bats.

Heavy-scaled and armor plated fish that once were native to our oceans. Dinosaurs, mostly smaller than those we had on this planet. Dolphins and whales are quite common in at least 3 solar systems we have covered, the planet Endo in the Rigel Centaurus solar system has whales much larger than the largest we presently have on Earth.

I understand that a very large planet, called Herculobus has dinosaurs at the present time that are at least 5 times as large as the largest we had in the past. We did not cover the star where Herculobus is one of its planets. That information comes from a limited edition book called "UFO contact from the Pleiades" by Col. Wendell Stevens, U.S.A.F. (Ret'd.), & one other source since. It is also interesting, if you go ahead and read the book, "Your Galactic Neighbors", that an oxygen-based atmosphere like ours is largely the most common, with regard to all of the planetary systems we have been describing in this book. The significance is that there must be not only sentient life out there in more general terms. It strongly indicates that this entire galaxy is absolutely and completely populated by sentient species of one kind or another.

What does all that mean to us? It means that we have been consistently lied to, and much important information has been kept out of our text books, etc., to keep us seriously ignorant. - Back to the mushroom business. . . . .

Other Civilizations Out There Have Been Described In Other Publications Since 1970:

The Paschat (Lionoids) of The Sirius A solar system, are mentioned in the book, "Our Galactic Neighbors". They obviously have had space travel capabilities for millions of years.

They originally colonized Sirius A, long before the Lyrans came along to get their permission to colonize Sirius B. The Paschat have been mentioned elsewhere, as well, so there is corroboration.

We can also mention the Zeta Reticulans, positive E.T's. who have been visiting this planet for thousands of years. The so-called "Grays", negative E.T.'s that made secret agreements with Eisenhower, are another example, and they come from the Constellation of Orion.

There is a race of tall, slim, and very pale folks who have been living in an underground complex in California for at least 300 years. They are mentioned and described by Dr. Richard Boylan.

There is another race of humanoids, said to be quite similar to us, who come from a planet referred to as "Koldas" said to be not far from this solar system. They apparently have been running out of food, or means to grow more of it. In any event, they have been mentioned by Col. Wendell Stevens, in one of his books, and also by Commander Haaton of the Pleiades Star Fleet, in the Phoenix Journals. As I recall, Barnard's Star was mentioned in Col. Wendell Stevens' book. There is a race of humanoids whose "blood" is chlorophyll. One of those was captured when the discoid craft crashed at Roswell, New Mexico in 1947, and the neat little fellow, referred to by MJ-12 as "E.B.E." (extraterrestrial biological entity), was held for at least a year and a half before he died.

The planet Venus is occupied, in its interior. I had stated earlier that the surface of Venus was devastated by reptilians from Bellatrix, about a million years ago. However, its interior remains intact and livable. I have printed photos from the internet, by N.A.S.A., showing polar openings on Earth, Venus and Mars. Much earlier in this book, it was mentioned that when Atlantis attacked China and the Atlantean rebels in the area north of Greece, just before the flood, Rama, a great leader from our inner world civilization of Agartha allied with China and the Atlantean rebels, to defeat Atlantis. Those inner earth folks are the same blood line from the lost continent of Lemuria, that came there from Sirius B, originally, with some follow through from Andromeda, a very long time ago.

To make a long story short, the Venusians are indeed there, and they are members of the Galactic Federation. Next to nothing has been said about any civilization of any kind in the interior of Mars. However, Richard Hoagland and others have laid out and explained much evidence of an earlier civilization on the surface of Mars, including its pyramid. The pyramid has been covered in far greater detail in dictated material from beyond this realm, and I have read about it in two sources. Photos of mars show the opening in its north polar area.

Getting back to the fact that all planets are hollow, you will find, when you read through the book "Your Galactic Neighbors" that a vast majority of civilizations, of all species covered so far, here and elsewhere, live in the interior of their planets. In most other planets we have covered, other than Earth itself, each of the planets described has a "firmament", consisting of one to three separate layers of ice crystals, in their stratosphere, a few miles up from the surface of the planet. In the past, in the case of Earth, our two layer firmament was set at 15,000 to 18,000ft., and 35,000 to 38,000ft respectively, above the surface of this planet. It also follows, and has been explained, that our present lack of a firmament, is why our Earth bound human race has had its life span reduced to 60 to 100 years, rather than 750 to 950 years as it was in the time of Adam. Also, we used to be as tall as the Sirians and Pleiadeans.

There is another humanoid group out there referred to as the "Verdant" They have a grayish skin color, and are exceptionally intelligent. Their solar system is far beyond our region, and they say it is about one third of the way across this universe of Nebadon, or Orvonton, as it has also been referred to. They have been written about in a book by Philip Krapf, a retired feature editor of the LA Times newspaper, who had been taken up into their mother ship, which has been parked in the sky for a long time, on the far side of the moon. The first of the two books he wrote is called "Contact Has Begun".

I will now make closing statements concerning so-called conventional publishing sources, and groups and clubs etc., involved with U.F.O's and contact, etc.

Near Total Suppression Concerning UFO's & E.T.'s:

All of the major media, including every major publishing house in North America and England, has been completely controlled by the Illuminati group and their minions since as early as 1954. Also, by 1954, all of the major broadcasting media for radio and television were at that time, and now remain controlled by Illuminati families. MJ-12, not long after it was set up, and more particularly after its security arm became the CIA, began to successfully infiltrate and influence U.F.O. study groups in the late 1950's. Many of the big names involved, were agents of, or paid off by the CIA and MJ-12.

To make a long story short, you would not find much of any truthful consequence in any of the major media, unless they had their own point to make, and wanted to sidetrack or lie to us. To my memory, and I have seen almost all of them, there has only been a half dozen or so of books on extraterrestrials and U.F.O.'s, even via private publishing sources, until 2001 -

2002 that are telling any kind of a true story.

Col. Wendell Stevens, (U.S.A.F. - Ret.) had investigated U.F.O. crash sites etc., since 1943. He investigated and covered all of the very detailed reports of Billy Meier of Switzerland, covering his long term contacts with the Pleiadeans. Billy took very clear photos of 3 or 4 models of their scout ships. Further to that, Billy was taken up in one of their scout craft, and out to their large mother ship, which he described. Billy was then taken on a tour in the great mother ship, and went on side trips with Semjase, his Pleiadean lady contact. On one of those side trips, he was taken down to a planet, where its people were at war, and already had anti-gravity craft. On another side trip, Billy was taken down to a massive planet called Herculobus, with dinosaurs at least 5 times the size of those we once had on Earth.

Col. Stevens risked his life by turning all of Billy Meier's very complete and detailed notes of his contacts and his trips into his first fascinating book. All of his information is accurate and correct as published. The first book that I have in our collection, is called "UFO Contact from the Pleiades". It is rare, as only 1,000 copies were originally printed. Col. Stevens was greatly harassed and bothered by the U.S. government after that book was published.

We have another book that was published about the same time, with Billy Meier's photos of at least 3 Pleiadean scout ships in full colour, and they are absolutely clear and sharp against their background. Nobody among all of the "authorities" who checked out the authenticity of Billy's photos could find any evidence of tampering of any kind. It is also of further interest to note that the Pleiadeans had made highly scientific and very detailed comments concerning the consequences of nuclear testing, the dispersal of our Ozone layer, and other things, as completely detailed by Billy, and put into Col. Stevens' book.

One fellow, who wrote a manuscript that was annotated by an

extraterrestrial, was assassinated a long time ago, around 1970. I have read his material, and as I remember, his name was "Carlos Allende". His body was found in his car, at a remote location, and he had been shot dead. That is shades of MJ-12, and their usual approach to such things since 1947.

He had a copy of a then recently published soft cover book on U.F.O.'s which had handwritten annotations and comments therein, by an extraterrestrial, concerning their anti-gravity propulsion systems, in particular. Somehow, one of his extraterrestrial friends, familiar with such things, had done annotations in pencil, correcting ideas and concepts on U.F.O. propulsion systems, and further described two common drive systems. One was based on mercury or mercury vapor, and high intensity magnetic fields, and another was based on a twin disc system, involving large numbers of magnets, where a generated high frequency magnetic field would neutralize gravity, or provide its own isolated gravity field.

It is interesting to note that by that time, John Searle, in England had done his anti-gravity experiments, and ended up with a two disc system, based on a one-sided charge (John was a senior apprentice at English Electric when he did his successful experiments). If anyone thinks that MJ-12 had not been aware of Mr. Searle's successful experiments by the time that Carlos Allende was being watched, they are out to lunch, or they have been sitting on their brains...

Those criminals had an unlimited budget, and could afford not to miss much that related to their areas of concern. Also, MJ-12 and its offshoots had already been back engineering extraterrestrial craft by 1958, four years after Eisenhower's meetings with the grays, and by 1970, they had enough propulsion system information in hand to know whether or not Mr. Allende was onto something rather important to their objectives. In general terms, those were the matters of controlling anti-gravity propulsion systems on this planet, or stopping, anyone who had any potential of matching their own level of competence in that general area. There is obviously deep concern by those folks about exposing our existing ability to go into space without cumbersome rockets, or acknowledging the existence of our extraterrestrial neighbors. The "space program" has been mostly a sham since 1962, to keep us ignorant of our fast-evolving and highly secret space travel capabilities. The U.S. & Russia both also have devastating space weapons.

References:
1. The Day after Roswell - by Col. Corso (U.S. Army - Ret.)
2. UFO Contact From The Pleiades by
    Col. Wendell Stevens (U.S.A.F.-Ret.)
3. UFO Contact From Andromeda by
    Col. Wendell Stevens (U.S.A.F. – Ret.)
4. Contact Has Begun - by Philip Krapf
5. You Are Becoming A Galactic Human by
    Virginia Essene & Sheldon Nidle
6. The Pleiadean Agenda - by Barbara Hand Clow.
7. The Explorer Race - 1996 ET's and the Explorer Race -
    1996 –
8. Explorer Race - Origins & the Next 50 Years - 1997 ---
The last three books, on the referenced list above, are an accurately published version of very important information, and technical data, dictated from beyond this dimension. No lies are involved, as none are allowed from or by the source(s) of the information presented. All such dictation was taken, and publication was arranged and copyrighted by Robert Shapiro, of Sedona, Arizona. (Light Technology, Publishing, Box 1562, Sedona, Arizona 86339.)

I had read about 40 years ago, that the Germans had begun to build anti-gravity propelled discoid aircraft in the early 1940's, and had succeeded rather well by 1945. In that earlier source it was said that their craft were based on information provided by the Pleiadeans in particular. As I had stated previously, that story can now be clearly corroborated, as rather complete articles have now been published on the website: http://www.rense.com . Those articles contain both diagrams and photographs of experimental craft, with no visible propulsion system. The last and most efficient model in their sequence looks remarkably similar to one of the older model Pleiadean scout craft as photographed by Billy Meier in Switzerland in the 1970's.

Chapter 7

ANCIENT HISTORY OF PLANET EARTH
(Before our politically biased, B.S. based history as taught in our schools.)

A.) The Past 35 Million Years - with comments - based on available info.

Years Ago   Most Important Development, Etc.

35 Million   First Etheric Intelligent Civilization
The time Lords and spiritual hierarchy of this solar system created an etheric (4th. - 5th. Dimension) grouping of angel - like life forms which were to act as an intermediary until the evolution of a more physically evolved sentient primate occurred, that would be or become the land - based guardian of Earth. (Toward your better understanding, the 4th. - 5th. Dimensional levels, to us are like our afterlife situation, where we are between lives and awaiting our next incarnation.) Eight million years later, a cetacean water - based primate had indeed developed, evolved to sentient status, and was beginning to develop a rudimentary civilization. At this point, the aetheric soul forms occupied the bodies of this race of primates, and they moved rapidly toward developing a far more complex civilization. (Aetheric becomes physical.)

26 Million   Dinoid Reptoid Invasion
Don't get carried away with the mistaken assumption that Reptilians did not have space travel 35 million years ago. They sure did, and began meandering across the galaxy that long ago. Humans, compared to the Reptilians and Dinoids are a Johnny-Come-Lately species, and evolved, first as an idea, and then through efforts of those Cetacean folks from Earth, a very long time ago, and that can come later on with the background.

Twenty six million years ago, two non-human civilizations came into our solar system and claimed it as part of their original creation myths which suggested that they, and not the other species, should control the entire galaxy. These folks were a Reptilian or Reptoid one from one of the lesser known stars in the constellation of Sagittarius, and a Dinosaurian or Dinoid one from the constellation of Orion. With no recognizable opposition, the Reptoids and Dinoids went ahead and established their respective colonies, on Earth, as the Pre-Cetaceans were continuing to evolve and develop a highly efficient agrarian civilization on their own, on a separate continent, at that time.

18 Million   Rise of the Pre-Cetaceans

The Pre-Cetaceans developed a highly efficient agrarian society without the use of technology, and began regularly trading with the Reptoids and Dinoids who each then occupied their own separate continents. The Reptoids and Dinoids, being very well developed and advanced technologically by then, created better technology for the Pre-Cetacians, who were then already more than capable of providing all of the agricultural product needs for those other two species. The three species civilization on Earth at that time was flourishing, with free trade and a good level of respect being shown each other, and they developed a large degree of cooperation on all levels. This was considered unusual, particularly by the Dinoid civilizations from Orion, who wanted to maintain Reptilian based exclusivity in the galaxy, and it was counter to their religion, or creation myth.

10 Million   Start of Orion Scenario

The Dinoids from Orion were very concerned about the situation on Earth, as their creation myth (and religion) suggested they, and obviously other reptilians were the only species that were supposed to be supreme in this galaxy, which was "created for them". In the meantime, the Pre-Cetaceans were trading their agricultural products with the Dinoids and Reptoids. That situation was working out to the advantage of all three species. The Dinoids from Orion were non - plussed by this development, and wanted to see if they could stop that situation from spreading in their empire. They eventually held a series of meetings with their Dinoid counterparts on Earth, and it was decided they would set up a plan of action to destroy the Pre-Cetacean civilization. The Pre-Cetaceans suspected something was going on, and through their priests etc., and by accessing the spiritual hierarchy, they determined what the Dinoids had planned. By that time, the Pre-Cetaceans had space travel and large space ships at their disposal.

8 Million   Destruction of Dinoid / Reptoid Group by Pre-Cetaceans

Once the Pre-Cetaceans knew what was going on, they got permission from the Earth's spiritual hierarchy to plan and carry out the destruction of the Dinoids and Reptilians, who now were working in concert toward the Pre-Cetaceans destruction. The Pre-Cetaceans continent contained what are now known as the Ural Mountains, in a North-South direction, and their fusion powered electrical power systems at that time were all situated inside those Ural Mountains. What they planned, and carried out, just after they got into their starships was the implosion of those fusion generators, which resulted in the destruction of all civilization then on Earth, including the Reptilian and Dinosaurian. Those Pre-Cetaceans from Earth then began a serious search for an advanced form of sentient primate, with the idea of obtaining, and then further developing a creature with a very practical body form and great potential for superior intelligence. The handwriting was on the wall for them, and they were about to deal with the reptilian challenge head-on.

It took them a very long time, but they found their candidate species on the third planet of the Vega solar system in the Constellation of Lyra. With the complete cooperation of the Spiritual Hierarchy, and the pre-cursor organization for what would later become the Galactic Federation of Light, they genetically altered that species over a period of time. They eventually came up with a completely sentient, and perhaps ideal humanoid species, with exceptional intelligence, and a high level of creativity. This result was deemed essential, as it would be necessary, in order to oppose those Reptilians and Dinoids. A superior humanoid race would need to have at least matching intelligence, if they were to be capable of matching and defeating the reptilians.

6 Million   Earth Recovering From Attack (on Dinoid / Reptoids)

In the meantime, up to this point, the new humanoid species, now called the human race, was evolving at a prodigious rate, on the third planet in the Vega solar system in the constellation of Lyra. They became space-faring in short order after that, as they had Earth's Pre-Cetaceans to assist them toward that objective. Space weaponry was developed, which could damage and destroy reptilian spacecraft. Now the game was on, and the reptilians and dinoids, being extremely intelligent, but totally logical and linear in their thinking and development, were now up against a race of beings who had the added advantage of being free thinkers and highly creative. New weaponry, easily capable of destroying reptilian and dinoid spacecraft was in the hands of all of the human star fleets, and those dinoids and reptilians were being fought to a standstill, every time they encountered a human Starfleet. This is being covered here, as it relates to those newly evolved humans who would colonize Earth.

4 Million   Galactic Federation of Light Founded - Earth Selected For Seeding

The Galactic Federation of Light was founded by the newly developed human race, which by then, had been migrating for a long time throughout this galaxy, and also into the Andromeda galaxy. Please bear in mind, at this point, that the Dinoids and Reptilians were representing the Dark side of this greater reality in which we all exist.

In the meantime, the humans were able to fight the Dinoids and Reptoids to a standstill by about 4.5 million years ago, and were continuing their migrations throughout the galaxy. This went on for about 2.5 million years, and by then, human colonies had spread to where they were very close to our solar system. The Galactic Federation of Light decided at that time to seed Earth with human immigrants. The spiritual hierarchy had also decided that our planet Earth was going to become the only planet in this galaxy which would evolve new life forms.

This solar system also was to be the training ground for souls, as to negative and positive, and would have both good and evil sides as far as the human race and its continuing evolution, was concerned.

2 Million   Hybornea Founded
The first colony, called Hybornea, also known as Hyperborea, would last for about one million years, and was a complete Lyran / Sirian type of civilization.

1 Million   Hybornea Destroyed
The Dinoids were aware, about a million years ago, that humans were then in total control of this solar system, other than Maldek, which still had a long established Reptilian colony.   The Reptilians decided to eliminate that problem. They destroyed Hybornea, along with human colonies on the surfaces of Mars and Venus, and re-established their own small settlements on Earth.   For a period of about 80,000 years, our solar system was held as an outpost of the Dinoid / Reptoid group.

900,000   Lemuria Founded
The humans of the Galactic Federation of Light brought a battle planet, called "Nibiru" into play, and directed it toward Maldek, the main home of the dinoid / reptilians in this solar system. Maldek was then destroyed, with its shattered pieces becoming the asteroid belt. With all of the reptilians gone from this solar system, it was decided to start up another model human colony. This colony was established on a then very large continent in the Pacific Ocean, now referred to as Lemuria.

As further points of interest, Nibiru is 29,000 miles in diameter. It has a very long elliptical orbit, extending all the way to the Sirius B star system, and Nibiru crosses almost through Mercury's orbit, once every 3,600 years. It is the 12th planet, as referred to in books by Zacharia Zitchin. Those books were based on the translation of over 2,500 clay cuniform tablets. Nibiru is referred to in the bible as "Wormwood".

**400,000 BC   Atlantis, Yu, and Libyan / Egyptian
                      Daughter Colonies Founded**
These so-called daughter empires thrived and continued to develop on their own.   However, Atlantis, being greatly scientifically oriented etc., decided that they should take over this planet, as they were superior to the Lemurians and were now in a position where they should take charge.   The Atlanteans, along with renegade groups of Centaurians and Pleiadeans laid out a plan. By breaking up and directing the fragments of one of Earth's then two moons to crash into Lemuria, they would destroy Lemuria, and would then become the dominant power on this planet.   That nefarious plot was successfully undertaken, with Lemuria being sunk into the sea, about 25,000 years ago.

**25,000 BC   Atlanteans Begin Forming And Con-
                      solidating Their Empire, Toward Eventual
                      World Control & Enslavement**
Somehow that situation was an ancient example of the present U.S. Government and its relentless progress toward that objective, since about 1932 ??? This large scale, mostly consolidated Atlantean empire would last for about 10,000 years, and it was the first truly hierarchical governing system in this world. This period was called the middle empire, and it eventually became the equivalent of a powerful warring dictatorship, much like our present system of things. The totally unjustified system in India, of the "untouchables", or extreme class distinction, is a carry-over from the Atlanteans. That kind of horrendous treatment of our fellow citizens was a common situation in all of the reptilian societies in the

constellations of Orion and Draco.

15,000 BC to 10,000 B.C.
During this period of time, the despotic Atlantean leadership and its interrelated "elite" groups decided to reduce the common people of this world, eventually, to the equivalent of slave status. This was carefully done by means of genetic manipulation, over a long period of time, and resulted in a human with only two operating strands of a twelve strand DNA.

What this achieved was to reduce the intelligence of the average human to a range of 2.5 to 3, on a scale of 10. The elite, and their other relatives in all of the other human occupied solar systems out there, would have an intelligence level of 8 to 10. The resulting average Earth human was also instilled with a strong desire to have a leader. This was deep-seated to the point of obsession with most of the genetically altered humans at that time. Eventually, as is happening here at the present time, a serious number of highly capable people from the Elite and ruling classes of Atlantis, became very disenchanted with the Atlantean rulers, who only wanted world conquest and the total enslavement of the rest of the world's population.

A group of them were exiled from Atlantis, and formed a very advanced, scientific and high tech settlement, which became a thriving region, known as Ionia. Their exile began a little less than 15,000 years ago. They had plenty of time to develop their systems of things, and had fully intended to re-establish the earlier Lemurian type of government, (similar to the original U.S. Constitutional Republic form of government where the individual citizens are sovereign) to replace the Atlantean system of conquest and dictatorship.

Much later, probably about 11,000 BC or a bit more recent than that, Atlantis decided to destroy Ionia. The Ionians quickly became aware that a strike by Atlantis was on the way. The complete story is far more elaborate, than what is being revealed here.

It now becomes rather interesting. If you are aware of, or have read the "Vedas" - from India, - English translation, or otherwise, you will read the story of the last battle, and what is being referred to, when Atlantis was defeated, through the use of discoid flying craft and rocket propelled nuclear weapons. (What's new in this world?)

In any event, what had happened, is that Rama, son of the king of Agartha, or Shamballa, our inner Earth civilization, had already established a thriving new civilization on the surface of this planet, now called India. Rama joined up with Horus, son of Osiris, king of the Libyan / Egyptian empire, and defeated Atlantis.

This planet is hollow and occupied on the inside. All planets, including ours, have openings at their poles, and a small central sun which supports the same types of seas, land-masses, plant and animal life as exist upon the outer surface of the planet. The thickest part of the body of this planet Earth is about 800 miles thick, in the equatorial region.

Following the destruction of Lemuria, the Yu Empire, which occupied a large area, presently containing part of China, and virtually all of India and Tibet, absolutely refused to become subservient to Atlantis, and made themselves clear in that matter. The Atlanteans, together with the Libyan/Egyptian empire (subservient to Atlantis), attacked and destroyed the Yu empire. Survivors from the Yu Empire fled to the inner Earth, taking their own then advanced technologies with them, and re-established themselves in Agartha.

At this point, Atlantis had been defeated by an alliance that worked out quite well, and things began to quiet down, as there no longer was anyone with an objective of world domination, busily bothering everyone else to achieve that type of objective. This situation went on for about 4,000 years, without any serious conflicts. Obviously, in the meantime, the new civilization in the India and Tibet region continued to evolve, and if they were anything like we have been in the last 300 years or so, their progress was very significant.

10,000 BC
In the meantime, a few talented scientists from Atlantis, migrated to Egypt, along with many others who wanted to get away from a civilization that only wanted to dominate and enslave other countries. This has been mentioned in Edgar Cayce's readings. Those talented people designed and built the great pyramid between 10,400 and 10.300 years ago, or close to that. In any case, it is essential at this point, that each major event in history should be placed in its proper sequence, before we go to the next events. The building of the great pyramid fits here in sequence.

Eventually, the Libyan / Egyptian empire was attacked by the Sumerians. They wanted to eliminate the last influences of Lemuria, by taking over the Libyan / Egyptian empire. This is a negative situation, but we must bear in mind that the Nibiruans were firstly and most seriously involved with the Sumerians after the fall of Atlantis, and the Nibiruans were only self-serving, wanted to be worshipped like Gods, and if they told the Sumerians to Crap there would be a great movement in the crowd, or if they told the Sumerians to go to war, guess what? = No surprises. - - - Same Crap. The mushroom business was well under way quite some time ago, and has evolved into a high tech. operation in more recent times ...

Horus, king of the Libyan / Egyptian empire was joined by Rama, King of India, at that time, and a series of conflicts followed. When they decided to destroy some of the crystalline towers holding up the firmament, each of the empires involved in the conflict thought that there would only be enough rain falling to flood out their enemy. However, the entire two layers of the firmament gradually came down, and resulted in the 40 days and 40 nights of rain, as described in the bible, and the flood destroyed the warring nations, and changed history in short order. The flood happened at about 6,000 years ago, in our time frame.

The firmament consisted of two layers of water (ice crystals), with the first being at an altitude of 15,000 to 18,000 feet, and the second being at 35,000 to 38,000 feet above the surface of Earth. Its purpose was twofold. Firstly, the average surface temperature of the planet was very stable, in the 70's Fahrenheit, and did not vary more than 5 degrees between the equator and the polar regions.

Secondly, the firmament filtered out virtually all damaging rays from the sun, and a human lifespan under those better conditions ranged from 750 to 950 years, as mentioned in the Old Testament. There is a firmament in place in virtually every other occupied planet in this entire galaxy. The firmament, in each case, serves to protect and energize surface dwellers on any of those planets.

CHAPTER 8

OUR MORE RECENT HISTORY - SINCE THE FLOOD

Remember the planet Nibiru? Guess what? Its main or primary citizens are said to be Reptilian / Human hybrids, the Anunnaki. Those members of the negative Satanic Anchara Alliance were seriously involved in the Atlantean leadership, etc., throughout their continuing history. The issues could be confused where we have said that...

However, we must bear in mind that many of the Pleiadean colonies throughout the galaxy were set up as defence colonies, to discourage or deal with the Dinoid / Reptilian menace that was so prevalent in their time. A Reptilian / Human hybrid was no more likely to want the murderous Dinoid / Reptilian types bent on conquest to enter their space, than would a Lyran / Sirian Human. At the same time, the hybrids also felt through experience, that they really had nothing to fear from humans.

The strange part about this whole exercise concerning Nibiru, is that the Nibiruans have said that they had been dealing with our humans on their own, aside from the Galactic Federation, as early as 450,000 years ago, where they had our earlier humans doing their Gold mining, in what is now Africa. They had to do that, in order to mine and process as much gold as possible. As a 4th. Dimensional race, they needed the gold in order to be able to access our 3rd. Dimension and to survive within this 3rd. Dimension.

This information concerning those past activities comes from explanations provided by Anu, the great leader of the Nibiruans. His comments are recorded in a book called the Pleiadean Agenda, by Barbara Hand Clow.

Until about 1994 - 1995, the Nibiruans belonged to the Anchara Alliance (The Dinoid / Reptilian-Satanic negative empire). Pleiadean / Centaurian rebels, involved with Atlantis prior to, and also in the destruction of Lemuria, probably were already involved with the Nibiruans, and were situated with them, on Nibiru for thousands of years.

We would have human Nibiruans, and those who would be the hybrids we have been discussing. There is nothing solid about this information at the present moment, and it would have to be referred to as speculation, until corroboration can be arranged. As a note of serious interest, at the present time, the Nibiruans are cooperating (Nov. 2007) with the good side here on Earth, and with our helpers from the Galactic Federation. They are assisting in the process towards arrest, and incarceration of the murdering leaders and manipulators of the illuminati banking cartels and their puppet govern-ments, including all of the present G-8 nations. The result will be world peace and the restoration of all of our personal freedoms, much as intended in the original U.S. constitution.

A reptilian **(negative)** form of government consists of a series of Kings, who each have a district, and the usual number was 10. One of those 10 kings would be chosen as the ultimate leader of the planet / solar system, or whatever. This is similar to the earlier systems which had been set up on Atlantis, where there was a series of kings, and in related writings the magic number was 10. In any case, what happens is that under the kings there was a fixed structure of district, state or regional "nobility" much like there was in Europe, in recent history, and below them, we have "common people". The lowest level was the "untouchables" or slave class, much the same as the situation in India, which was so difficult to change for such a long time.

As long as you are being filled in on the situation as it applies to the reptilians, let's take a look at other galactic humans and their types of civilizations. A human **(positive)** form of government, as carried forward from Lyra, to Sirius, and subsequently to dozens of other constellations in this galaxy, is generally laid out as follows: At the individual, family and local community level, it is a clan type of system, where there are 6 to 12 clans represented, where each clan specializes in a particular type of skill and profession, such as Engineering, Science, Administration, Cultural History, Science Engineering, Spiritual Warrior, etc. There is a general council system, where each clan council holds an equal voting position on the main governing council, which acts as an over-all governing unit of a planet, or even an entire solar system. Every individual citizen, in all cases, is totally sovereign. The governing council is in the position of serving the needs, goals or supporting achievement (s) for the good of the entire civilization.

All individuals are expected to apply their creativity and skills toward the greater success and progress of their family, clan, government, and civilization at large. Those galactic human civilizations eliminated money-based economic exchange systems a very long time ago. Our modified system of world government, which will be set up in the very near future, will retain a new precious metals backed world monetary system for a while longer, until we evolve to the point where money will no longer be needed, and matters of hoarding and greed will also tend to phase out. Achievements will be rewarded with honors and status only.

The Nibiruans, and this has lots of corroboration, have been behind our reptilian forms of government on this planet more solidly, since the time of the flood, and have been the creators, and then the directing motivators behind our negative satanic group on this planet (the "illuminati"), who remain in control of our Earth civilization at the present time, but without their Annunaki overlords as directors.

The Nibiruans held regular meetings with representatives of the Anchara Alliance, who were treating this planet as part of their empire.

The illuminati have been behind, and have controlled every significant government on this planet, almost entirely, since the flood, and that remains the case up to the present moment. They are behind the infamous "Skull and Bones" and "Scroll and Pen" societies at two of the most prestigious universities in the U.S., and their tentacles extend similarly, to universities in England, Canada, and the rest of the British Isles and Germany and probably also throughout Western Europe. They are also behind Satanism. The illuminati have also been in control at highest levels of the Freemasons, and are included in a majority sense in the Jesuit order, where their black pope controls the regular pope in Rome.

Much has been written about this situation, but not published or publicized by main-stream media or publishers, as they are controlled by the illuminati. Some of the best and most complete background information and details have been written by David Icke, of England, including his most complete book, "The Biggest Secret."

Look it up. It is a real eye opener. David Icke has avoided assassination by having incriminating VCR tapes, photos and other information placed in a number of locations with trusted associates, for open distribution if any attempts are made to assassinate him. It is fascinating to learn what he has said about the British royal family, and other royalty and powerful families in England and Europe being Satanists and participating in animal and human sacrifices etc.

Also, we must now add in the matter of the power mad Atlantean rulers revving up their massive crystal generator, and directing its energy downward, in an attempt to devastate the Yu Empire (China, Tibet & India). That situation backfired on them, causing massive earthquakes, followed by subsidence, and much of Atlantis subsided into the sea. Our present governing idiots in the U.S. in particular seem to be similarly foolish and don't think they would face any consequences at their level for the damage they are doing to other people and to the planet itself.

Plato, in his writings, circa 360 BC, brought up the 10 king situation, always common with the reptilian system of things. He told quite a story about Atlantis that his contemporaries, with their then level of skills, ships and technology could not confirm or deny, or do anything else about. Plato's writings referred to as his "dialogues" seem to be stories of "Timaeus and Criteas". They can be looked up, and checked out. Plato, obviously, had some connection with sources of carefully hidden records which by his time, had been stored away for a long time.

Chapter 9

ANTI-GRAVITY CRAFT, INCLUDING INTERNPLANETARY MODELS BUILT FOR U.S. (One World Order) SECRET GOVERNMENT

In laying out this particular information, I am not giving you anything new, or based on my own observations. As usual, I am simply providing information that is out there at the present time. The information is current, like available right now. If you want far broader and more complete coverage of the following information and statements, please access the references provided.

Available Information May Be Old Information

Although you might have had odd hints here and there from privately published articles and books, what you will see in our controlled publishing media will be rather sketchy and more often than not, very old. In November of 2000, Popular Mechanics identified the TR3-B as the Lenticular Re-entry Vehicle, a very large nuclear powered anti-gravity craft. Were the readers of that article made aware of the fact that just such a craft had first become operational in 1962?

This particular situation is much the same with regard to ET communications, free energy devices and systems, along with all of the more complete realities of physics, quantum mechanics, and the real truths of history. What you see is what you get, and much of what you see and are fed in our media are half truths or empirically developed lies of rather good quality. This appears to be particularly true when we are dealing with space, anti-gravity systems, E.T.'s, and anything related to those subjects which could be connected back to our government (s).

Palatability? - The truth may be much harder to swallow than the lies.

Here are a few true statements that you might find to be unbelievable or unpalatable, depending on how completely mushroom-conditioned you are. .

1.)   The Germans had built and tested as many as 7 discoid anti-gravity craft "Vril" prototypes, before the end of World War Two, by 1944 and the last one had exceptional performance, (their greatest secret) by the end of the war.

2.)   The Germans had also already built and tested their first time machine by that time. (Later on, the U.S., being related to consequences of The Philadelphia Experiment, followed up to total success in the Montauk Project)

3.)   The first ET U.F.O. recovered by the U.S. government came down in 1941, west of San Diego, and was retrieved by the U.S. Navy.

4.)   Lasers, Night Vision Technology, Light Emitting Diodes, and superconductivity are among the items of technology back-engineered from the ET craft (flying saucer shape), which crashed in the Roswell area of New Mexico in 1947.

5.)   An ET person, called E.B.E. (extraterrestrial biological entity), said to have come from the Zeta Reticulum solar system, was kept in secure confinement, under orders from MJ-12, from 1948, until "EBE" died in 1953. His blood system consisted of chlorophyll, and he could only eat plant or vegetable types of food. Apparently, he had come from a planet with a lower Oxygen and higher Carbon Dioxide type of atmosphere, where plants would thrive. This does not belittle the fact that they could travel across the galaxy. Intelligent? Seriously so...

6.)   President Jimmy Carter had been briefed on Extraterrestrial matters, and related documents covering that briefing in detail, were eventually leaked. One page was missing, and an insider with MJ-12, admitted that the missing page describes an individual of joint ET-human heritage, who emerged 2000 years ago, to try to end human violence. The insider confirmed that this person was the one referred to in the Bible as Jesus. (Adam was also a hybrid.) - confirmed by the most recently recovered scrolls, written by Judas Iscariot, Jesus' scribe.

7.)   The U.S. secret government is aware that our star visitors traverse the galaxy by manipulating space and time. Time is reduced to almost zero, and acceleration is increased to infinity. (Remember the "wormholes" in the Star Trek series?)

8.)   The U.S. government's slow pace of disclosure about UFO reality, is like a balancing act. Free (zero point) energy, and all ET technology would then come in, all at once. It must now be borne in mind that the governments of virtually all developed nations are under control of the same Illuminati based group of individuals. Also, their planned total enslavement of the human race has to be a total surprise carried out in secret, until they finally declare "martial law" under some contrived pretext for its justification.

It would hurt the stockholders and thieving management in obsolescent industries, and the multinationals don't want to lose their power, along with dictatorial control of our governments - in our western part of the world, in particular.

Advanced Anti-Gravity Aerospace Craft - Based On Back-Engineered ET Technology
This information was current in 2005. The confirmable and currently accessible source of this information will be provided at the end of this section.

There are presently three means of gravity neutralization and anti-gravity propulsion, as being used by our dark side folks. It appears that the ET's were being careful, like we as adults might be, when we hand our brats a box of firecrackers, or teach them how to make a big bang, using simple science..

The first, and most primitive method is **electrogravitic,**

where we use millions of volts to disrupt the ambient gravitational field. This results in an 89% +- reduction in gravity's hold, accordingly reducing the weight of the craft also, by that amount. This system is used on the B-2 Stealth Bomber, and the TR3-B Astra Triangular craft. (These will be mentioned later, in our list of presently operative anti-gravity, or hybrid craft with anti-gravity systems built into their means of lift and propulsion.)

The second system is **magnetogravitic**. This involves generating high energy toroidal fields, spun at incredible rpm's, to disrupt the ambient gravitational field, to the extent that a counterforce to Earth's gravitational pull is generated.

It was suggested to our main reference herein that the secret Nautilus spacecraft uses magnetic pulsing, which appears to be a version of this particular technology.

The third system is **direct generation and harnessing of the gravitational strong force.** Such a strong field extends beyond the atomic nucleus of element 115, which of course is not supposed to exist according our established science. By amplifying that strong force, and using anti-matter reactor high energy, and then directing it, it is possible to lift a craft from Earth, and then change directions by vectoring the shaped antigravity force field thus generated. We are now going to give you an outline of existing speed and performance potentials of transatmospheric, and ultimately inter-planetary craft produced and operated by the secret government of the U.S., which were currently in use in 2005.

The B-2 Stealth Bomber. This is a low-observable, strategic, long range heavy bomber capable of penetrating sophisticated and dense air defence shields. It has an electrogravitic system on board, and that relates to why it was so expensive to build.

The Aurora X-33A. This is a moderate sized space-faring vehicle. The Aurora can operate on conventional fuel and anti-gravity field propulsion systems. Aurora can travel to the moon. (The U.S. has a small station on the moon, and also on Mars. - This was also mentioned a long time ago in a spoofed, restricted and virtually banned book called ALTERNATIVE THREE.)

The Lockheed-Martin X-33A. This military space plane is a prototype of Lockheed's other space plane, and has electrogravitics on board.

The Lockheed X-22A. This is a two man anti-gravity disc fighter. It can fly into outer space. It has been said that the X-22-A anti-gravity fighter disc fleet is equipped with neutral particle beam directed-energy weapons, and can use optical and radar invisibility, and is now deployed for worldwide military operations.

The Nautilus is another space-faring craft, a secret military spacecraft which operates by magnetic pulsing. It makes twice a week trips up to the secret military intelligence space station, which has been in deep space for the past 30 years, and manned by U.S. /U.S.S.R., now CIS military astronauts.

The TR-3 "Pumpkinseed" is a super-fast air vehicle. Its fuselage is oval, and shaped like a pumpkinseed. It appears to be using pulse detonation wave engine technology, and has a top speed in the order of mach 10, at 180,000 feet altitude.

TR3-B Astra - This is a large triangular anti-gravity craft within the U.S. Fleet. It was used in Iraq, in the Gulf War's early hours, with electromagnetic pulse cannons. Its effects were absolutely devastating, and burned its human targets to a crisp, instantly...

It seems that as far as our One World Order folks are concerned, the matter of killing our fellow humans is no more complex or morally bothersome than shooting clay pigeons.

Northrop Antigravity Disc. (The great pumpkin) - This is because it has a reddish-orange glow, emanated by its energy field. These were first test-flown in 1992, and have obviously been further developed since that time.

The XH-75D or XH Shark antigravity helicopter was an oddity at the time it was described in 2005, and not much more is currently known about this craft at the present time, in 2008.

The TAW-50 is a hypersonic antigravity space fighter-bomber. Its capabilities are jaw-dropping, and it includes most everything learned since the first back-engineering began in 1955 or so. Its top speed is in excess of mach 50, and that has been called a "conservative estimate". We are looking at speed beyond 38,000 miles per hour, and that is in the atmosphere. Gravity escape, or orbital speed is close to 25,000 mph., so the TAW-50 is obviously a space vehicle.

Beyond what has just been said here, there is much mention made in the referenced published material about the horrendous military and death-dealing potentials of this last, and other previously described craft.

These are now in the arsenal of our so-called governing group, who are more quietly referred to as our "One World Order".

Ref.: Main Source Material for Anti-gravity craft = http://www.drboylan.com

Chapter 10

QUESTIONS & CONCERNS -
PROGRESSION OR REGRESSION?

The questions that come up are: Why do we have to make war? Why would ordinary people like us create war, and are the other folks out there in this world out to get us, or likely to start a war with us? I think not.

And now, why was, or is, war necessary in the first place, except to satisfy the ego of some despotic individual (s) or group (s). ???

Such people have no spiritual or moral values. They are totally self-serving, and have only personal gain to achieve as a so-called "elite group", at our expense. "We the people" appear to be satisfied to call those murdering criminals "our leaders"?

What are the common citizens of America going to do about this present situation? - Don't get carried away with assuming that only the U.S. is involved in this situation. The U.K., France, Russia and other countries have been aware at top secret levels all along, and Russia, for instance was about 10 years ahead of the U.S. by 1980. The mushroom situation is common in all of the so-called "developed" countries, and exceptional control of our western media has further kept the other seemingly less important countries completely in the dark in the meantime.

Have we degenerated to the level of morons, idiots, sheep, lemmings, or what? All of these questions are now being more commonly asked by increasing numbers of disillusioned Americans, along with increasing numbers of close by Canadians and many others in the developed countries who are also beginning to wake up from their contrived and imposed state of ignorance.

More of us Canadians are becoming rather completely aware of the bullshit and what is really going on, and surely wish we could do something about it, and change the world some way for the better. However, control by Khazarian Zionists and dominating industrial corporations, is primarily in the U.S., secondarily in England, and thirdly in Germany at this moment.

The Khazarian Zionist Bolsheviks killed (murdered) 66 million people in Russia, between 1917 & 1990 +-, so you could assume they are a powerful bunch of bastards. They have been totally supported by the world's bankers, including particularly the Rothschilds and the Rockefellers. Once you have a better grasp of what has really been going on, you may see things differently. You may not be foolish enough to assume that anything those folks are supporting or running is going to do us any good, or is designed in any way to do anything other than enslave us within a totalitarian system under their absolute control.

Generally speaking, our complacency toward the One World Order is better established in Canada, than in the U.S. Canada currently tends to be more like Western Europe who now "seem to" be comfortably tolerating their enslavement.

The situation is sure as hell apparent at this moment, where: (a.) Our Canadian leadership is part of the set up for a North American Union of Canada, U.S. and Mexico, including new valueless North American single ply toilet paper $$$$ dollars, and neither the Canadian media, our Canadian government, or our pious politicians have bothered to keep us informed. - and - (b.) The law is still on the books in Canada, where only our Canadian Government and our "Finance Minister" in particular has any right to print money in Canada, and our politicians have quietly conceded that right to the bankers, to loan us our own money with interest, with no law to back it up. We Canadians are the biggest suckers of all.

U.S. politicians screwed their voting citizens long ago, in 1913, and made that situation the law in the U.S., where they gave their country to the bankers, who would eventually own it through compound interest and a contrived "national debt" - For what? To whom? and why?

U.S. presidents Washington, Jefferson and Jackson, in particular, warned against the plot, already in the works in and from England in their time. Later generations of politicians, willing to be paid off, sold out their country. In the meantime, to be sure of getting a proper foothold, the British started the war of 1812, where Washington was sacked, with the real purpose being the successful elimination of any record of the 13th. Amendment to the U.S. constitution in its original form. Americans should read it, to get a better handle on criminality in their own government, and the original set-up allowing that to happen. They should also become aware also that the BAR Association is really the "British Accredited Registry".

The 13th. Amendment was to prevent anyone with any direct connections to royalty or any foreign government ever being elected to public office in the U.S. Anyone with such credentials as banned by the 13th. Amendment, also could not be a citizen of the U.S., and certainly could not hold public office. Now, the real questions are: who's who, and what's what, and where do I fit in, if you are an American citizen. (Don't forget that the Khazarian Zionist Bolshevik's really are not citizens of any country, and don't care about you, and yet they control your country?)

As this book and its contents evolve, you will at some point, recognize the extent and breadth of

Chapter 11

WHAT'S COMING DOWN THE PIKE?
PREDICTIONS - ENERGY ETC...

A.)   A lot of things have been said about alternate energy sources, and in a more current sense, Hydrogen seems to be tantamount to many of those discussions. Academics are closer to sheep or lemmings than most of the rest of us. They are supposed to be taking their students into the future. For the most part, they are stuck in the past, and think their most fondly held theories and pronouncements should be absolutes. That tends to make them appear to be invincible. To my way of thinking, they are probably only constipated in most cases, and their usual excrement will follow in the near future.

B.)   When we look at Hydrogen, and the matter of splitting water into Hydrogen and Oxygen respectively, that is all well and good. That has been done for a long time, quite successfully, but the limitation has always been the level of efficiency. Hydrogen is the main primary output of that process which fuels your car, or whatever, and after the recombination takes place, this leaves water as the residual coming out of the tailpipe.

However, when we look at Brown's Gas, we have Monatomic Hydrogen and Oxygen. Four times as much energy is available to the burning process, and the end by-product out of the tailpipe is Oxygen. That changes the scenario.

Automotive and larger scale applications and uses of Brown's Gas have been discouraged for a long time. Its detractors have been saying that Brown's Gas is exceptionally volatile, and highly explosive. So is gasoline. Gasoline is far more powerful than dynamite. In the earlier section of this book on suppressed inventions & technology, if you review the story of the fellow who made Brown's Gas, long after Dr. Brown invented it, and then used it to run racing boats, he was smart enough not to have a problem with it, but others apparently did not want him to have it or use it. Try money and control as the real reasons. . .

Anyway, the way Brown's gas will be used to fuel vehicles is where it is continuously generated on a measured scale that is adequate, and passed on into the intake manifold of your car. Bingo! You will go 100 miles on a couple of hundred milliliters of water. I see the small associated problems being solved, and that Brown's Gas will get applied to automobiles on a larger scale in the near future. The toughest problems will be bureaucrats (parasites) watching their tax based gravy train disappear.

C.) When we look at the potential interaction between electromagnets and the most powerful of our present "ceramic" magnets, we have free energy potential which will blow our high priced One World Order criminals out of the water.

There are already quite a number of electromagnetic impulse motors out there, and they are all said to be "over unity". That is B.S., as there is nothing over unity in such an arrangement. The 150 pounds of push or pull in each of those high powered ceramic magnets, and all that the inventors (including me) have had to do, is drive the darn things with timed impulses from properly placed electromagnets. When those inventors are no longer being shot for making such things, we are going to see a lot of them out there, and they could easily become one of our main sources of free energy. They are simple to make, and can be designed to put out massive amounts of power.

D.) Solar Heat Panels are soon going to have a very large market wherever we have a winter season. I remember a local inventor, just south of Calgary, who was heating his large home right through to April, in 1978. He had built and installed solar heat panels on the long south facing roof on his barn. He stored the heat in cleaned up high volume gasoline tanks, salvaged from filling stations that had been abandoned or shut down, in the fast growing city of Calgary.

He had buried those tanks deep underneath his house, and insulated them as thoroughly as possible. At the present time, we have better materials and manufacturing processes etc. available for making highly efficient and high quality solar heat panels.

E.)   Solar electrical energy panels: We are going to see their efficiency levels climbing to where they will be in the order of 20 to 25+% efficient. However, far more importantly, we are going to see their cost drop from the present level of as much as, or more than $6,000.00 per kilowatt, to where they will sell for less than $1,000.00 per kilowatt. We will see better combinations of organics and crystals involved in those panels. They will pick up a broader range of light energy, including levels of UV and infrared which are not being adequately accessed by our presently more expensive technology.

F.)   We will soon see the gradual adoption and eventual manufacturing of solid state free energy generators. The zero point energy generator that was patented in the U.S. on March 26th. of 2003 and suppressed ever since, is going to come out, probably before the end of 2008. There will be other free energy devices provided by some of us other inventors and our extra terrestrial friends. Our ET friends will follow through as soon as they are satisfied that we will no longer be creating and fighting wars. They do not pollute the environment on their home planets and they don't want us to do that here either. Everything in this universe affects everything else, and the closer recipients of the negative energies are going to feel it more intensely than those farther away. It is those closer folks that are now dealing with us, and trying to do us some good.

G.)   In 2008 or 2009, we can expect to be introduced to interstellar communications technology, where we can instantly communicate with our space brothers and sisters many light years away. Expect that one for sure, and it is really definite, when we learn that a U.S. inventor had managed to create just such a thing before 1950 .... (T. Galen Hyeronemous)

H.)   Inter-dimensional Portals - We will be able to locate those, and there are a few of them on this planet. They will eventually be used, as we grow in awareness. This may be beyond the comprehension of most of us for the moment, but we will become more generally aware of it in a few years.

I.)   Replicators - We will see these things in most of the extraterrestrial mother ships that come to this planet in the next few years. They involve the equivalent of 6th dimensional holographic projection, and have already been explained in a book called "The Nature Of Reality", dictated by ascended Master Hilarion to Maurice B. Cook, of Toronto, in 1979 - 1980.

When you, as a thoroughly brainwashed victim in our present scheme of things see my comments about replicators, you might realize and remember, based on what I have said much earlier in this book, that the vast majority of us humans have an intelligence level of 3 on a scale of 10. As you observe our galactic neighbors, at 10 on that scale, and their performance, it must also be borne in mind that they are more than a million years beyond our level in terms of science and technology. Many of our academic experts are going to look like a bunch of retards by comparison, and our concepts, following such observations, are very likely to change. Also bear in mind, that intelligence levels and the Richter scale are somewhat similar. A person with an intelligence level of 3 may be able to relate his or her level by saying that if you square 3 you get 9, and if you have to relate that to a 10 you are going to be dealing with 100, compared to 9.

Chapter 12

HOW BIG IS THE MUSHROOM PROBLEM?

Those who haven't woken up by now, are in for more surprises, in connection with ordinary things that affect our daily lives.

Agriculture:
This category includes environmentally damaging and soil depleting chemical fertilizers, which had been proven to do those things by 1913. How this happens is that the chemical fertilizers tend to kill off the soil bacteria to begin with, followed eventually by the earthworms.

The end result is that the plants cannot assimilate any minerals, because the minerals have to be "chelated", for any measure of absorption to take place. It is the soil bacteria and the earthworms that chelate the minerals enabling the plants to assimilate the minerals.

It is an absolute fact that the food value in vegetables that are produced in a purely organic fashion, with properly composted and recycled vegetation leftover materials can have twice the food value of vegetables produced through the use of chemical fertilizers. The reason for this is that the soil bacteria and earth worms are strongly supported by the application of the composted material, and anything else that will provide them with a good source of the nutrients they require.

Earthworms and soil bacteria, as I said before, are the real means of assuring that plants can assimilate essential minerals that result in an absolutely healthy end product. It seems obvious that the purely profit-oriented management of corporations serving the agriculture industry are looking at net dollars of profit at the end of the exercise, and don't care at all for any other considerations.

I have a friend with his masters in biochemistry, and he has told me that the valence electrons of atoms of organics and inorganics turn in different directions. Inorganics are a problem, for that apparent reason, and assimilation is limited. He was suggesting that situation for us humans. The situation with plants also appears to be the same, when we compare the results of using composted materials and keeping the earthworms and soil bacteria at abundant levels.

Further to those things, there are probably very few if any herbicides that have no effect on the environment. Also, insecticides are often far more damaging to our birds and animals which normally eat insects that are killed by insecticides. As far as birds are concerned, the American Eagle became extinct in the U.S. because of DDT, and had to be re-established, with birds from Manitoba and Ontario in Canada.

There is a falcon in Canada, that feeds during the summer season on prairie ground squirrels which Canadian prairie folks call gophers, and in the winter, they feed on grasshoppers in Argentina, which has had a problem recently, with grasshoppers. They sprayed insecticide, in 2005 & 2006, to kill off the grasshoppers in Argentina. The falcons ate the grasshoppers and died by the thousands.

Under our present system of things, we have a corporate government. Within that arrangement, the corporations that manufacture and sell chemical fertilizers, herbicides and insecticides are not facing any consequences for killing off so many species or our native birds and animals, and they apparently do not care at all. This crap has been going on for a long time, and as far as I am concerned, it has to stop.

A majority of us must stand up and say **No!** to the use of those chemically based things. We should also refuse to buy or consume any grain or vegetables not purely organic. The only thing those people understand is money. They will cooperate as soon as we quit buying their products and they start going broke. I expect that in the near future, following the NESARA announcement, and the change of our legal systems back to common law, we will be able to bankrupt those corporations with class action suits.

Everything on our beautiful planet is interdependent with everything else, and those at the top in the corporate end of things apparently don't care about that. It seems to be only a matter of how much of that stuff can be sold to our farmers and others who don't really know, or are lied to about the consequences.

Why is this happening in the first place? Our agricultural schools are set up so that the chemical companies who make the fertilizers, herbicides and pesticides and provide bursaries etc., are the ones who dictate what is taught in those schools.

Ref: Secrets Of The Soil, by Jonathan Winters & Christopher Bird, also Silent Spring, by Rachael Carson

Bread & Wheat & Rice:
Away back in time, the business and commerce types (the Pharisees - 13th. Tribe) - not related to the original 12 tribes of Israel - Khazarians - they also became the Russian Bolsheviks, and are now also referred to in the U.S. in particular, as the Zionists. They set up a plan to take over Babylon. It was a subtle and very successful long term plan, over a period of two or three generations. They traded white flour (with all of the husk and bran etc. removed), to the Babylonians, and advertised white bread as the greatest of the latest.

With all of the husk (fiber - bran) and wheat germ removed from the wheat, the B-vitamins essential to nourishment and sustenance of the brain, were sharply reduced or completely removed. The people of Israel continued to eat their whole grain pita type of bread, maintained their intelligence, and eventually the Babylonians no longer had the level of intelligence essential to maintaining and governing the

Babylonian city empire, etc., and Israel took over. Please remember that those parasites were Khazarians, and not the original Hebrews.

There is no essential difference between that situation, and what we of the present generation are putting up with. In our case, the added inorganic chemical items in junk food at most of the North American fast food franchises such as Kentucky Fried Chicken, MacDonald's, Swiss Chalet, Wendy's and others include bleached white flour in bread, macaroni and spaghetti etc., with the added bonus in many cases, of poisonous chemicals such as food coloring, MSG, nitrates, sulphides and sulphites, aspartame, aluminum compounds, and other subtle poisons, and excess sugar in our food. All of this is pushed, supported and distributed by corporations, who are also running our present governments, and dictating approvals (probably through massive payoffs) of poisonous sweeteners and food additives by the F.D.A.. This continues to be the case, in spite of serious proof of poisoning by Aspartame, Monosodium Glutamate, micro-wave, food colors, hydrogenated oils, and numerous other items, some of which are also obviously carcinogenic. **Breaking News:** Early in 2008, the news is now out that the head of their FDA equivalent in China, was recently shot by firing squad. It appears that he, like his American counterparts, was open to bribes from the pharmaceutical companies. He apparently took a bribe of $800,000.00 +-, and the Chinese Communist government found out about it.

When it comes to rice, millions of people were killed off a long time ago, by a disease referred to as Beriberi. This is probably the world's largest case of corporate murder, as imposed on the Far East, with China probably being hit the hardest.

That situation was relentlessly and murderously subtle, just like imposing white bread on the Babylonians. Beriberi is a deficiency disease, where the b-complex vitamins are removed by a polishing process, to form "white rice". Isn't it interesting to note that nobody was ever charged or made responsible for the mass murder of millions of people?

The meaning of Beriberi in the large two volume 1949 edition of Funk & Wagnall's Dictionary is as follows: "An organic disease of the peripheral nerves, characterized by partial paralysis, swelling of the legs, and general dropsy : due to the eating of polished rice, or specifically to the absence of vitamins of the B complex. " Even though it would be considered a matter of digressing, rather seriously, there is something that bothers me about all of this stuff, particularly Beriberi in its historical context.

*Historically, within that same general time frame, there was a Committee of 300, consisting primarily of the banking and royal families of Europe. The rest of them were their cronies who were into the general conspiracy up to their eyeballs. In their time, they were the original One World Order. **That particular group, in their** time, introduced Opium to China.

Unbelievable? I guess so, for someone who has not been paying much attention. However, that situation is absolutely true!!! The money has the clout, the clout has the power, and damn near all leaders, politicians and judges etc. can be "bought". Once the first "buyout" has been done, their individual alternatives are zero, and once the controllers know that the individual knows what is going on, assassination is on the agenda for that public figure, if they are likely to defy "the establishment".

***Ref:** "Diplomacy By Deception" by Dr. John Coleman.
"Secrets Of The Soil" by Jonathan Winters & Christopher Bird.
Also, check fourwinds10.com and rense.com re: MSG,
Aspartame, etc.

Poisonous Food Additives & Cookware & Methods Etc.:
If we go all the way back to the 1920's, it was already known at that time that aluminum cookware could be a serious problem. The crux of the problem is that aluminum is highly conductive, and any measurable amount of aluminum

ingested, eventually, over time, affects the central nervous system of the human body, and begins to short circuit its functions. It had already been proven to be a key causative factor in Alzheimers disease, senility, serious memory loss, and other central nervous system disorders, in the 1920's. Isn't it convenient, and it surely was far more profitable that the aluminum companies, although probably well aware, didn't do a damn thing about it, through the remainder of the century.

Common table salt in hot water will readily leach serious amounts of aluminum into solution. Now you know why such a high percentage of our earlier generation folks became senile by the time they were into their 70"s, with the problem getting progressively worse.

Microwave cooking is dangerous and damaging. Russia had banned microwave ovens as early as 1947. By then, their research had shown that microwave cooking demolishes the molecular structure of any food cooked by that method. The consequence is that very little of the nutritional value of the food can be assimilated by your digestive system. You think our corporate government and our corporate media who are major controllers of our governments should be making us aware of that? Not likely. Those folks prefer to lie to you, and subject you to brainwashing until you are brain-dead, to maintain absolute control.

Anytime you go for coffee at your popular coffee shops, in all of them you will have a marvelous opportunity to put aspartame or one of the other artificial sweeteners into your coffee. Aspartame in particular has been completely proven to be as bad as or worse than rat poison. It causes central nervous system damage like aluminum, and has a broader range of effects and will cause those problems within a shorter time frame. Not many people are aware that the chemical formula for aspartame is the same as for nerve gas..? There is a deeper and more sinister story about that product which was approved by the FDA in the U.S., in spite of having been proven highly poisonous before being approved. The head of the FDA at that time, for having proven himself "faithful to the cause", would eventually move on to a higher level in the U.S. government. His name is Donald Rumsfeld.

Our next item on the menu is far more common and probably more insidious than aspartame. Monosodium Glutamate which has been put into our canned soups and hundreds of other canned and off-the-shelf food products for many years was also proven, a long time ago, to be a slow acting, but very efficient poison. Extensive research has proven that MSG progressively causes brain damage, along with other forms of damage to the central nervous system of the human body. Hundreds of major corporations in the food business are using it every day, as the most important function of MSG is that it is a flavor enhancing substance, which fools your taste buds into believing that something tastes much better when MSG is present, even if it would otherwise taste stale.

Now, let's look at other common things containing chemical products that can make you sick by causing internal body damage over time. The effects of such things tend to be empirical cumulative, and not readily noticeable in early stages, but they are there nevertheless. We have nitrites etc., in our meats, like bacon in particular. We have sulfites in many other food items, as well as in our wines.

You might ask, what's the big deal with all of this? I have a most interesting friend who has his master's in biochemistry, and he is an inventor, and has come up with this world's most efficient leaching solution chemistry for gold and platinum-group metals, and it is totally environmentally clean.

With his superior ability to make observations and deductions, he noticed something in particular, and I found that most interesting. I am repeating here that he suggested that the reason why we seem to get less food value out of artificially or chemically created food items, is as follows: In the case of the chemically created item, their valence electrons are spinning in the opposite direction, and that seems to spell the difference between organic and inorganic. It is like negative and positive, or acceptance and rejection. He could be right, but that has not been proven yet.

Why do we still have chlorine in our domestic water supplies, when the Europeans have banned it from their systems? Chlorine is a surplus by-product from our aluminum refineries. Chlorine is the chief cause of atherosclerosis. =Massive damage to the blood vessels. That has been known since 1963.

Fluoride, in Canadian water systems is an exceptionally poisonous by-product of the uranium industry, and also turns up with aluminum. The original story of Fluoride being good for maintaining your teeth is an absolute lie. It causes slow continuous brain deterioration. Check it out on http://www.fourwinds10.com.

Building Materials & Concrete:
Without looking any further than at what I have personally observed over the last 30 years, indications are that the building materials and concrete industries are where many of our one world order cats have locked themselves into a darn good deal. They have progressively set up and further consolidated and expanded a series of extremely powerful monopolies. The key elements are sand & gravel pits & deposits along with the production of Lime in particular, and now further expanding heavily into vibracasting of bricks, blocks, slabs, walls etc. and obviously at the same time, creating monopolies and setting and controlling the prices of all those things.

This is sure as hell not for your benefit or mine, but it is a goldmine in each case, where excess profit is the general rule. As time progressed, one could easily observe the takeover of virtually all of the Canadian lumber companies in British Columbia. The situation started out with an embargo by U.S. interests. The Canadian lumber companies lost much of their market, and the largest world scale companies in the U.S. bought out virtually every large Canadian company.

It all interrelates to complete the circle, and force most of the construction business to buy their primary and most essential materials at premium prices from those interlocked and international conglomerates.

Where I am now, next to the extremely fast growing City of Calgary, which has housing prices in its main core area in the top 7 in this world, I have seen the price of concrete far more than double in the last 20 years, and more than triple in the last 30 years.... Why is that?

Let's look at one situation that relates directly back to the mushroom business and who runs what. The Jesuits control the Mafia, and the Mafia controls most of the concrete business throughout North America. It looks like the Illuminati are behind that monopoly system, as it surely is with many of the others, like the energy field in particular.

Isn't it bothersome that in the U.S. away back in the 1920's and 30's if you were to check things out, there were laws referred to as "antitrust laws" where the matter of setting up conglomerates or monopoly groups to control the market, and the prices paid, was generally prohibited. After the legal system in the U.S. went onto the Uniform Commercial Code after 1932, the U.S. became a corporation with a corporate form of government. - One thing leads to another - In retrospect, it seems obvious that the earlier antitrust situation was really B.S.. It was set up by our controllers to keep their own competition from doing what they themselves intended to do, all along, and what they have far more recently done, to the point where they now also have total control of the government.

Drugs, Pharmaceuticals & Medicine:
Old John D. Rockefeller proved very completely in his day, that if you want to eliminate the competition, all you had to do was sabotage the competition, or destroy their facilities. (if you could not buy them out to assure absolute control). That situation was already established by about 1910, when old John D. went big time, into the pharmaceutical business, and began buying into, and buying out pharmaceutical businesses. Old John D. just couldn't turn down the idea of 3000+% profits on pharmaceuticals....

In our medical schools, the pharmaceutical companies have determined what has been, and continues to be taught. Our medical students are completely duped in the process. The students will not generally be made aware of studies proving that the organically inert and poisonous prescription medicines produced and sold at ridiculously high prices by those pharmaceutical companies are more often making people sick rather than well.

They are also not made aware that the objective of the pharmaceutical companies is only to provide things that will alleviate symptoms, or deaden your ability to feel pain. Their products are not designed to "cure" anything. As a matter of fact, if you become an M.D., and you pass on the message that you can cure anything, you can be ejected from the "medical association".

Who really controls the medical association, the medical and agricultural schools, and any of our other schools? - Chemical & Pharmaceutical companies!

Hydrocarbons:
What about why our hydrocarbon fuels, which are so ridiculously expensive, have not been replaced, and do not face any direct competition from other far more efficient things like forms of Hydrogen, and a large number of free energy systems invented since 1903? Also, why don't we have highly efficient solar heat panels to any extent in the northern

hemisphere? I suspect it has something to do with those same people and their control of all of our so-called "conventional" sources of energy, which have not changed very much in the last 75 years. - And also their control of what is taught in our schools.

This is probably the biggest farcical, lying situation we have faced in the last 75 years. The main reason at this comparatively late time in history is that the petroleum industry at large controls the U.S. government, through what is being referred to as "petro-dollars" and obviously most other countries of the present world are capitulating. Why is that? The petroleum industry is largely controlled by the Rockefeller banking and corporate empire, and more recently, within as well as outside of North America, by the Rothschild banking and corporate empire. Those two family groups mainly, are Illuminati, at the top end. They also control the One World Order, all put together in one small package, with a few internally controlled and interconnected groups of lesser consequence thrown into the same pot.

When you are looking at two closely associated groups or families who control both the petroleum and banking industries, or in the majority, those folks really control the world at large. Control of money and energy is effective world control.

You have already read about oil and gas not being the consequence of swamp grass and gasses and other decaying plant life and organic matter that decomposed and eventually ended up in the sedimentary layers. I did say much earlier in this book that the real and unlimited source of such hydrocarbons is the highly compressed methane etc., that once was the atmosphere of this planet many millions of years ago. As the planet was evolving toward its present status, a great deal of that gaseous material was absorbed into the mantle Over time, and under adequate pressure by overburden, it became concentrated liquefied gas, petroleum, or petroleum distillate, trapped under the first basement or granite layer of rock, now situated below what we call the sedimentary layer, or sedimentary basin, as it is referred to in the oil and gas industry..

Subsequent cracks in the granite mantle due to earthquakes and plate tectonic motion and action, allowed some of the entrapped hydrocarbons to migrate upward though cracks or fault lines into the sedimentary layers. Where there was a rather hard and impervious layer above such an occurrence, a new entrapment was created, and the accumulated hydrocarbons would become the oil and gas deposits that are now our oil and gas fields.

I am not trying to be some kind of hotshot smart cat when I say these things. The Russians had proven that situation to a great extent in the 1930's, and in more recent times have drilled into the mantle, and ended up with oil wells that flow at high pressure, yielding in the order of 6,000 barrels of crude oil per day.

Our totally controlled media has not reported that Russia is now producing more oil per day than Saudi Arabia, and most of that oil is coming from below the first granite layer, referred to as "the mantle".

At this point in time, Vladimir Putin, president of Russia, has thrown the Illuminati out of Russia, and told them that they are not going to control his oil and gas industry like they have been doing everywhere else in the world. They are smarting, and furious, and Putin does not give a damn. Darn, Darn, Darn. Isn't that awful???

We haven't smartened up to any extent since, as the same satanic folks in the Illuminati and the One World Order group have been making very sure that no such information is released to us ordinary people. Within the framework of "their system", we only exist for the purpose of being their chattels and slaves, as they continue their illusion of being "the elite", who are convinced that they are "superior" .

It is the previously mentioned top end folks in the Illuminati who own and control a majority interest in all of the major oil and gas companies, and beyond that, more importantly, at least 75% of all of our oil and gas refining capacity. If you take a serious look at that situation in the real world, it would soon become obvious that it doesn't matter who owns the producing companies if you own the refining facilities, as the ball stops there at the last stage before the market, and at that point, the refiners own the output, and at the present time, also own and control the largest retailers in that business. There is now a controlled price structure all the way from the refiners to the final market, and we can't do a damn thing about it ... Doesn't that bother you, just a little bit ? Everything is sold to the retailers at a controlled price... Looks rather familiar, doesn't it? Those hypocrites at their filling stations make a point of mentioning how much tax is included in the price of your gasoline. To make it funnier in the world of smoke and mirrors, who really controls the government???

Here is another slant on the strategic ownership, manipulation and control of oil and gas reserves and production and prices in a political sense. Oil and gas reserves, and production etc., are more matters of enslavement and control, and to be used strategically, than to serve the citizens of the U.S. and / or Canada, or anywhere else for that matter. It is a matter of fact that enough oil reserves were discovered on and off the north slope of Alaska, back in the 1970's, to provide for the needs of the U.S. at that time, for another 200 years. Confirmation of that fact is available in a book called **"The Oil Non-Crisis" by Lindsey Williams.**

Precious Metals:
Guess what? The same things are true in the mining and precious metals business. The same group of Illuminati connected folks control a serious majority of the mining companies producing and dealing with all of the precious and strategic metals. Also, in connection with the precious metals in particular, they have until now, controlled all of the refining

processes, even if they have had to kill to get there.

As a key example of the tightness of control, a Canadian fellow who was recovering platinum group metals by means of his own processing skills, out of black sands in the Similkameen area of British Columbia, was assassinated in Nevada, many years ago. The name of that person was J.S. Wisdom, and in terms of creative intellect and useful inventions he was head and shoulders above most of his peers in his time.

I would not have been aware of that situation, except that I spent about 11 years working in the area of extractive metallurgy. There was particular emphasis on the platinum-group metals, and one of the most interesting small text books written on metals detection and identification had been written by J.S. Wisdom. He had been recovering, refining and selling platinum group metals, and was one of the first in North America who was not a member of the "cartel".

Those crude bastards killed him by running over him with a truck, close to his lab location in Nevada. "Freak accidents" of that type have happened, when it came to dealing with those who were bucking the system.

A Look At Our Severely Limited Educational System:
ES-1) The second law of thermodynamics is bullshit, and has been totally contradicted and proven seriously wrong many times in the last 100 years.

ES-2) Newton's law of gravity is backward. Gravity is a push and not a pull, and this was clarified in material by Walter Russell. - Suppressed - See ES-3 below.

ES-3) Maxwell's Unified Field Theory & equations were suppressed 150+ years ago, and Hertz and a couple of others excluded this from future text books etc..

ES-4) Our periodic table, as presently in use throughout our educational system, and in general terms by everyone associated with chemistry, is very inadequate. It has been practical for the most part, for its time, but it is not complete or correct. There are about 160 elements, without fooling around with odd isotopes, etc. All elements come in pairs which are male and female respectively. The new periodic table was laid out by Walter Russell in the U.S. in about 1926, along with rather complete explanations of the functions of continuous creation itself. This included the relationships between electricity, magnetism and gravity. Those explanations include a serious number of diagrams, such as the nature of gravity waves, etc... We were not supposed to learn or to know this???

ES-5) History as taught in our schools has been a continuously adjusted and modified story of all cycles of epochs, kingdoms and governments. This has been largely for purposes of justifying the controlling gang of scumbags as set up and supported by the Jesuits / Illuminati. I am led to believe that our real history is radically different from stories of kings and so-called heroes who could just as easily have been despots, dictators and murderers.

In the most basic sense, this world and the human race at large, has not needed wars at any time. That situation includes all of Europe and certainly also many other countries including Israel, for the last 2000 years. For instance, who has been told in our history books that the Rockefellers and the Rothschild's financed the Russian revolution, and that virtually all of its set-up, and that it was controlled from England?

Aeronautics & Space Travel:
We have been totally limited and restricted in both of those areas. Firstly, the big boys controlled the manufacturing of aircraft, so who are you going to sell your own new inventions to in that business? Also, it was and remains their own domain, as to whether or not a new approach is accepted by their closely connected cartel of manufacturers, tied back to the governments they control - like a closed circuit system.

In matters of spacecraft and anti-gravity propulsion, or gravity neutralization, all accumulated information from ET vehicles which have crashed on this planet since 1941 has been classified and suppressed. That technology has since been reverse-engineered, and has been totally controlled by the Dark Side - One World Order - Government, as to building its own anti-gravity spacecraft.

All of this has been set up to enable them to more completely control us ordinary citizens in their process of creating a more complete enslavement system. That subject has been covered rather broadly in previous pages, and does not need any further attention here.

How Did They Tie Down The Electrical Energy Business?
Back in Tesla's time, when he had been doing his research on being able to send electrical energy without wires, far beyond where it was generated, he did indeed achieve his objective. Some of his earliest experiments showed that he could send that energy for 28 miles with virtually no losses. Shortly following those experiments, his big project at Wardencliff on Long Island, New York, was forced into bankruptcy, and that spelled the end of electrical energy being available at long range from its generation point without wires.

It is a shame that we see all of those electrical power transmission lines leading into and looped around all of our cities and towns of any significant size. The reason for that is that it represents the monopoly on that power by the utility involved. It occurred to J.P. Morgan early on, in Tesla's time, that it would be necessary to own and control the electrical energy all the way from its generation point to the customer's premises, and to then be able to measure and record its use in order to make the customer pay for it.

Free Energy?

Virtually all of the bullshit imposed on us that there is no such thing as free energy, is just that - bullshit !! and really nothing else! For instance, water power is free energy.

It is only a matter of harnessing it in some manner. The same applies to electrical energy, and a number of inventors have already been shot in North America after demonstrating free energy devices.

In spite of a deliberately lying and totally controlled media, the real truth is that there are vast numbers of so-called "free energy" inventions out there, ranging from gas mileage improvement up to 500%+, to a series of self-propelled electrical energy generators, and many other things to achieve the same advantages. I already have inventions involving extreme gas mileage improvement, and free electrical energy. That does not make me unique at all. Those things are logical to a conceptual inventor, and quite a number of us have figured those things out, and a serious number of prototypes have been built.

The only things keeping those "new" things out of your range of observation is intimidation, suppression of information, government expropriation, and in some cases, destruction of the prototypes and assassination of the inventors.

Cosmic Science?

I have mentioned that Walter Russell came up with a new periodic table, together with a rather complete explanation with illustrations and diagrams showing how our universe is structured, energized, empowered, and follows certain immutable laws that we were never made aware of...

Cosmic Science, with its explanations and diagrams is laid out in book #137 of the Phoenix Journals series, now available for reading or downloading on the website http://www.fourwinds10.com.

All of the explanations etc. were dictated by St. Germain, to Walter Russell, who recorded all of the information, until the entire series of subjects in that large presentation was complete.

Cosmic Science changes a few concepts and contradicts theories now accepted by conventional science as absolutes. We can start with gravity. Gravity is a push and not a pull. What we call magnetic energy is really "gravity energy", and from that primary energy form comes both magnetism and electricity. A magnet is called a "gravity bar." A magnet has 4 poles, not just 2. Gravity wave energy permeates this entire universe, and in order to harness it properly, we must use different coil shapes, etc. The reason for this is that the gravity energy exists in the form of spirals - hot to cold, and back to hot, causing and sustaining such effects throughout this universe, etc...

Who Or What Is Behind The Suppression of Knowledge?
The Illuminati, One World Order, with its secret governments, secret science, and black budget operations has been totally aware of Cosmic Science since at least 1926, if not sooner. Since that scientific knowledge is essential to understanding and creating anti-gravity devices and free energy types of electrical generators, we have been limited in those areas. However, at the same time as we recognize and mention those things, some of us free thinkers have come up with free energy generators. The One World Order folks have shut us down, locked up our patent applications and even shot some of us to make sure none of us could mess up their absolute control of our limited systems of things.

It is more than bothersome that such a small number of criminals have been able to set up and maintain a system capable of suppressing us, keeping us under their absolute control, and jailing or killing us whenever necessary to keep their own control mechanism and its management intact.

The matter of keeping important and pertinent information

secret, as it concerns principles of science and reality, elected representatives, and other subjects necessary to the clear understanding of this world by us ordinary citizens is a serious matter of concern. We have been kept completely ignorant of very important concepts, ideas, facts and developments. You will see my later reference to Maxwell having conceived a complete Unified Field Theory (1854?).

The illuminati are also at the top end, the real "Zionists". Fools from our various churches who call themselves Zionists, are mesmerized by that term, assuming that it simply means that they were descended from the original Hebrews. That may be the case. The illuminati, who identify themselves as Zionists are really what were, and are descended from the Pharisees, who were of the 13th. tribe, which were Khazarians from northern Russia, and Mongolia, and not Hebrews.

*Ground rules followed by the illuminati are known as the Zionist Protocols, and simply reading them might make you want to throw up. They would take up 60+ pages. -**"Behold A Pale Horse" by William C. Cooper**, covering things from UFO's to the "Secret Government" & CIA, etc. has a chapter with all 24 of those protocols printed out in full format. They fit what has been really going on.

In the scheme of things, they are (the illuminati) the ones who control the Freemasons, at very top levels, as well as The Skull and Bones Society, the Scroll and Key society, and others in England and Europe at large. - and of course, the Pope in Rome. (Controlled by the "Black Pope" of the Jesuits.)

If anybody thinks the Jesuits are dedicated to support the sovereignty of the ordinary citizens of this world, they need a strong dose of the hidden truth about those Satanists. (Eric Phelps is an author who has exposed those criminals from top to bottom. - Look him up on the internet.) The truth is very shocking, to say the least. Those innocent looking criminals are at the top of what is referred to as the One World Order, and they, most of the time; decide which president or politician must be assassinated to keep the progress of the illuminati toward a slave society intact.

I have not said much about the Annunaki, who are reptilians living on the planet Nibiru. It is interesting to note that there were roman copper coins minted 2000 years ago. The symbol on the back of those coins is the 8-pointed star of Nibiru. The Nibiruan reptilians like those in the Orion system, and two other major constellations (Draco & Sagittarius) were members of the Anchara Alliance 25 million years ago, until 1994-95, in our time.

In 1994 -95, Satan, in his/her female embodiment, referred to by those reptilians as their god, Anchara, decided it was time for peace in the galaxy, and made that known to her "subjects". This soon led most of them to later join the Galactic Federation. With that having been said, it should now be mentioned that <u>we here on Earth have had a reptilian form of government throughout all of our recorded history so far</u>, and much farther back in time, to Atlantis, where that began.

The book of revelation in the bible refers to 1000 years of peace beginning at the end of our current era. The Annunaki have joined the Galactic Federation, and abandoned their control and direction of the Illuminati. That is what it was really referring to, after 25 million years of aggression by the reptilians, toward enslaving or destroying any other sentient non-reptilian races and cultures in this galaxy.

The only serious attempt to bring this planet back to a human form of government, resembling any of very large numbers in many of our surrounding constellations, was with the original American Constitution. It has been all but dead, and seriously ignored for more than a hundred years, and totally bypassed since 1932. Functionally, the American and Canadian legal systems changed over to statute law, based on the Uniform Commercial Code. (Completely Corporate Government.) Also, subtly, at the same time, our common law courts became Admiralty Courts, where the citizen is treated as a foreigner, and guilty until proven innocent. If you ever care to check that one out, look for the "Admiralty" gold fringe on the flag hanging in the courthouse.

All of these machinations were done in favor of maintaining the reptilian form of government, where the government has and holds all the power, mostly without answering to the people, and that format eventually leads to the total enslavement of all of its common citizens within the framework of a police state. This format means government by monarchy systems, elite groups and corporations, severally and collectively.

The secret leaders and perpetrators hide within secret societies, and go for total control of media, and of virtually all information exposed to the general public. A fascist system is created, and a complete police state evolves before the citizens realize it has happened. That situation is now quite noticeable, if you would care to take a serious look.

Remember what I said earlier? A Socialist dictatorship is called Communism. A Capitalist dictatorship is called Fascism, and the lies by either of those systems to their people, are to convince them that their society is benevolent, supportive, protective and best for their comfort and survival. In both cases those lies are total bullshit, and only a parasite or retarded dunce would be pleased with being a citizen of the system, if anything better was observed or available.

It was mentioned in the Book of Revelation in the Bible, and I have said previously, that at the end of this millennium would come the beginning of a thousand years of peace. (Don't get me wrong here. I don't belong to any church and would not even consider that. Churches are controlling and political, and don't really appear to be truly spiritual at all. The "church" as such has been a key element in total control of all of this world's population by the Illuminati, as led by the Annunaki.

That situation, based on available information has been in place for at least 2,000 years.)

The book of revelation is in the "truth and facts department", as far as I am concerned, having been dictated from the other side of this reality. It surely would have been eliminated if the big boys would have realized its potential significance in our present time frame. That "thousand years of peace" was apparently referring to this entire galaxy, and not just our little planet Earth.

Now, in 2008, on this planet, certain things are beginning to happen which will lead to the collapse of the Illuminati, along with their corporate forms of government as they now exist in most major countries. The greatest potential for dealing with those satanic fools has appeared on the scene just recently. In the year 2007, in the month of July, the Illuminati were already squirming.

Chapter 13

ILLUMINATI THREATENED WITH EXTERMINATION BY CHINESE RED & GREEN SOCIETY FOR CREATING DISEASES TO KILL ASIANS

New formidable opposition has already served them with an ultimatum, where trickery and disobedience will place them all on an extermination list, starting with their leadership, at the top. Up to this point they saw themselves and their organized systems as "invincible".

A certain Canadian born gentleman, by the name of Benjamin Fulford, who is a writer and investigative reporter, has become an integral part of this new situation that has the illuminati backed into a corner. Mr. Fulford finished out his university in Japan, and is fully conversant in Japanese, and familiar with the cultural situations in Japan as well as neighboring asian countries. He has written 15 books in Japanese, which have been selling well. He has a radio show, and also contributes to Japanese magazines.

In his most recent book, he brought up the matter of the secret government as run by the illuminati in the U.S. having created the SARS virus, and the bird flu. Recent solid evidence had confirmed that those manmade viruses are very specific to Asian genetics, where almost all fatalities have been Asian folks.

Mr. Fulford laid out all of this information in that latest book, and it recently came to the attention of the Red & Green Society. It is a secret society of Asians, originally and primarily Chinese. In1949, they were quietly backing Chiang's Chinese Nationalists. The nationalists were defeated by Mao Tse Tung and his Communists, backed by the U.S., and controlled by the Illuminati. By then, the Red & Green society was already a very old, well established and very secret organization. It is more tightly secretive than the Freemasons, and the illuminati. The society quietly moved its headquarters to the island of

Formosa, where it now remains.

Mr. Fulford, shortly after publishing the book, got a phone call from a Japanese fellow, asking him to meet at a hotel. Benjamin was told that the Red & Green Society had already completely checked out his information concerning the manmade viruses, and had found all of the information to be genuine. It was suggested that the society would like Benjamin to represent them in dealing with the illuminati. He was also then asked if he would go to Formosa to meet with the senior leaders of the Society for further discussion of what he was to present to the illuminati, as they now intended to take action against the illuminati.

Mr. Fulford went to Formosa. He met with senior leaders of the society, and was quite surprised to learn that a high percentage of them were businessmen and professionals. They told him that they wanted him to deliver an ultimatum to the illuminati, where they would have to guarantee to stop the spread of the man-made viruses, and meet a few other mandatory conditions as well, if they wanted to survive at all.

Mr. Fulford was told that the Red & Green Society has more than 6 million members, including 100,000 assassins. They were aware that virtually all of the membership structure of the illuminati included only about 10,000 people, and the Red & Green Society already had a complete list of all of them, and further knew that the illuminati has no list of the membership of the Red & Green Society.

Mr. Fulford followed through and delivered the ultimatum to the illuminati, and told them to go ahead and check things out if they thought the society was not likely to follow through. The ultimatum included the fact that if the illuminati did not follow through with the terms of the ultimatum, the society would start killing them, beginning with their top leadership.

The illuminati had already responded, and Mr. Fulford included their suggestions in an article published on the rense.com website, on August 14th. 2007. On reviewing that illuminati response, it looks to me like they are jockeying for position, and trying to buy time.

I think those jerks have got to go, so they will quit murdering people in Iraq and Afghanistan, and stop extending the suffering and starvation they are also responsible for in Africa and other areas. The red & green society gets my support for sure, as their philosophy is benevolent and not dedicated to dominating or enslaving anyone in or outside of their society.

There are many dozens of other areas where the mushroom problem exists big time, so it is redundant to continue with individual areas of concern. I will now fill you in on some other things which relate to the overall situation. They will relate somewhat directly to what has been going on, concerning larger issues we are able to observe at the present time...

These following items represent from time to time, rather short or long term things which we are gradually becoming aware of, each in its main subject area, as pertinent to our present day situation... Some, more bothersome than others...

Chapter 14

STAR NATIONS GAVE THE ILLUMINATI WARNINGS REGARDING RADIATION AND POLLUTION DAMAGE TO PLANET EARTH & THIS REGION OF THE GALAXY

This momentary digression is a matter of proving a point as far as advice and notices by our galactic neighbours is concerned. There have been a serious number of warnings directed at the illuminati, by local star nations, concerning :

1.) Nuclear bombs and nuclear fission devices of all kinds.
2.) The destruction of the rainforests in Brazil, and other places on this planet.
3.) Serious atmospheric pollution related to the use of hydrocarbon fuels, from coal to oil to natural gas.

I have read a very lengthy, scientific and detailed warning by the Pleiadeans as delivered to Billy Meier of Switzerland in the 1970's, and published in a very well written book by Col. Wendell Stevens, U.S.A.F. retired, and it would have been a very well laid out university lecture on the related subjects. His book is entitled "U.F.O. Contact from the Pleiades" Only 1,000 copies were ever printed as far as I am aware. My wife and I are book hunters, and like a couple of bird dogs, we located the book in Calgary, and bought it, - not cheap, but certainly worth it. Incidentally, she and I have done the same thing all the way from San Diego to Vancouver and Victoria, to Winnipeg, and most places in between, like Vegas, Reno, etc... If you want all of the best books to complete certain collections including those on U.F.O's, and to be able to afford most of them, go to the used book stores. You will find fascinating books that you never imagined, and the adventure will turn out to be fun most of the time.

Here is one of the earliest, and yet a typical example of the information that has been passed on to all of us, and we might have seen and read it, except for the illuminati control of our media.

Thirty Years ago, back in 1977, the "Ashtar Command", which is a command unit of over 300,000 starships of our Galactic Federation, cut into and overrode the British Broadcasting System, and provided a carefully worded message for all of us, along with our cold blooded Satanic leadership. The regional headquarters of the federation for our immediate district is located in the Sirius B solar system.

They had decided it was time to make an announcement to our leadership, concerning issues effecting both the health and safety of our planet, and which could extend farther out into the galaxy, to also effect other solar systems.

That announcement was made by a person named "Verillion" of the Ashtar Command. Although serious attempts were made by the secret government to block the message, it was completely recorded at that time, and finally, once again presented on the internet on August 16th. 2007, to confirm that it had been given 30 years before that point in time, and had obviously been ignored by our so-called "leaders".

Here is an admonition that seems to make a lot of sense, in case an extraterrestrial comes up to you and asks you to take him or her to your leader: Make sure you take along a large bundle, say at least 6 or perhaps more rolls of toilet paper, because in our present state of affairs, your leader at the top end is very likely to be an asshole.

Here is the message: For example, in most recent terms, the U.S. congress approved, and passed by more than 90%, certain fascist type legislation that virtually no sane American voter would ever approve of, or accept. I have only made this last couple of comments so that you will realize that the blockage and elimination of the message from Ashtar Command was not in the least unusual, considering how we have been governed for the last 70 years or more, fed the usual bullshit, and certainly **kept in the dark.**

Here is the Message:

"This is the voice of Vrillion, a representative of the Ashtar Galactic Command, speaking to you. For many years you have seen us as lights in the skies." "We speak to you now in peace and wisdom as we have done to your brothers and sisters all over this, your planet Earth. We come to warn you of the destiny of your race and your world so that you may communicate to your fellow beings the course you must take to avoid the disasters which threaten your world, and the beings on our worlds around you. This is in order that you can share the great awakening, as the planet passes into the new age of Aquarius."

"The new age can be a time of great peace and evolution for your race, but only if your rulers are made aware of the evil forces that can overshadow their judgments. Be still now and listen, for your chance may not come again. For many years your scientists, government and generals have not heeded our warnings; they have continued to experiment with the evil forces of what you call nuclear energy. Atomic bombs can destroy the Earth, and the beings of your sister worlds, in a moment. The wastes from atomic power systems will poison your planet for many thousands of your years to come."

"We, who have followed the path of evolution for far longer than you, have long since realized this - that atomic energy is always directed against life. It has no peaceful application. Its use, and research into its use, must be ceased at once, or you all risk destruction. All weapons of evil must be removed."

"The time of conflict has now passed. The race of which you are a part may proceed to the highest planes of evolution if you show yourselves worthy to do this. You have but a short time to learn to live together in peace and goodwill. Small groups all over the planet are learning this and exist to pass on the light of the dawning of the new age to you all."

"You are free to accept or reject their teachings, but only those who learn to live in peace will pass to the higher realms of spiritual evolution. Hear now the voice of Vrillion, a representative of the Ashtar Galactic Command, speaking to you. Be aware also that there are many false prophets and guides operating in your world. They will suck your energy from you - the energy you call money, and will put it to evil ends giving you worthless dross in return."

"Your inner divine self will protect you from this. You must learn to be sensitive to the voice within that can tell you what is truth, and what is confusion, chaos and untruth. Learn to listen to the voice of truth which is within you and you will lead yourselves on to the path of evolution. This is our message to our dear friends. We have watched you growing for many years as you too have watched our lights in your skies. You know now that we are here, and that there are more beings on and around your Earth than your scientists admit."

"We are deeply concerned about you and your path towards the light and will do all we can to help you. Have no fear, seek only to know yourselves, and live in harmony with the ways of your planet Earth. We of the Ashtar Galactic Command thank you for your attention. We are now leaving the plane of your existence. May you be blessed by the supreme love and truth of the Cosmos."

Please bear in mind that this particular message had been recorded by many at the time it was presented, and has also recently been presented on our marvellous internet. That means you don't have to take my word for anything, and ignorance is not an excuse, and not paying attention is not going to excuse anyone from ignoring the facts in this particular case.

That situation made me very pleased, as I have had the hardest time even paying attention to people who themselves have never paid much attention to anything, and yet they say "I don't believe that" - so what? My point is that you probably haven't paid attention to anything in particular, since you left school, and a controlled and lying media has been your source of information since that time.

Your "Great Leaders" have made sure that you know next to nothing to begin with. The consequence however, is that when we refer to any subjects they do not want us to know about, we are very likely to know nothing. In the typical case, the reaction is likely to be ego based, and has nothing at all to do with your mentality. You have simply been kept ignorant, and don't want to be exposed as being seriously unaware of what's going on. It is also very difficult to concede that your "Great Leaders" have been a bunch of unprincipled lying criminals who have had no sincere interest in your prosperity, or even your survival, and they have been bought and paid for by the illuminati and their offshoots.

Ignorance of what is and has been going on in the world around us is not necessarily bliss. It is more likely to be a state of zero, or numbness. That is until we face the consequences of not even knowing what to expect as our own future evolves. As they planned, those criminals would turn us into the absolute slaves they intended us to be, not just in the present subtle form.

The bottom line is that we have been fed bullshit and kept in the dark.

Chapter 15

WHAT ABOUT OUR LEGAL SYSTEM(S)?

The so-called laws in the U.S., Canada, Britain, and the United Kingdom, at the top end, and most other countries after that, relate only to the Uniform, or Universal Commercial Code, which is only "Statute Law" and not "Constitutional Law", or "Common Law" (English Common Law, based on the Magna Carta), upon which your concept of constitutional law would relate to..

To add insult to injury, as far as your personal concepts might relate in the U. S. in particular, your lawyers must belong to the BAR Association to be able to practice law. Guess what? The BAR Association is the British Accredited Registry, and being a member of that organization just denied an American lawyer his citizenship and right to be elected to any position whatever in any level of government in the U.S.. (13th. Amendment to the U.S. Constitution) - It says in general terms that any person who accepts any connection to royalty, or to any foreign government, fits that situation. Does this tell you something?

Like, maybe, you are being governed by traitors who have been, and continue to be committing treason, completely and continuously all the time, and you think those (bought and paid for) representatives of yours don't know what they are doing - to you? Sorry, mushroom, you are being screwed all the time, not just some of the time.

If you at any time would come before the court to face some charge. Ask the court for Jury Trial. Unless you are dealing with a "Capital Crime" your request will be totally refused. In Canada, there are even special "courts" which deal with Revenue Canada (IRS) issues. Jury trial would blow those parasites out of the water, and there is no way they want that to happen.

The income tax is unconstitutional in Canada, and not passed by congress in the U.S..

If you want to nail those folks down to facing personal responsibility, prepare an "information" in legal terms. This charges the IRS employee, or other bureaucratic person with having committed a particular offence under the "Criminal Code", in Canada. There are plenty of those chargeable offences being performed every time those folks come after you. Watch them scatter and look for their rat holes when you lay those charges. Charge the individual perpetrators personally & directly. – Bureaucrats will behave like cornered rats. You either negotiate and settle to your satisfaction, or proceed until they back off.

One of the problems however, is that you can't use a lawyer. The lawyer has a series of problems to surmount before he can honestly serve your position.

Under the U.S. Constitution, and / or under the British North America Act, he cannot serve you as a citizen of either country, as anything but a British subject. U.S. citizens do not realize that the lawyer's BAR Association, is really the British Accredited Registry. The lawyer is working under the banner of a foreign country, and under the U.S. constitution, he cannot even be a U.S. citizen if he in any way serves a foreign organization or country. In Canada, if he does not toe the line as far as the government is concerned, he can lose his BAR Association membership, which usually means his right to practice law.

If you, without being a lawyer, are smart enough to prepare your case properly, and also know how not to concede jurisdiction to a paid off judge acting on behalf of a foreign power, and acting under Admiralty Law, where you are guilty until proven innocent, you will get away with it..

The system of things is nearly impossible to circumvent. It has been more and more completely convoluted and complexed over the last 230 years. It currently appears that only a paid off flunky to the system knows anything about how to make it work in your favour and not in "theirs". We have done it, and won, after a fashion, in monetary terms, and they have been more careful, and no longer resorting to fabricated assessments. - Intimidation works until you fight back.

That exercise took a great deal of intense study and effort, plus a lot of valuable advice from highly aware individuals in 3 provinces, and "our technicality" turned out to be as important as theirs. In our seemingly unimportant case, Revenue Canada not only kept us in their "private courtroom" situation, but they also had the judge fly to Calgary from Montreal. We were not supposed to make waves, and their special mousetrap was set up to avoid that possibility.

The bothersome bottom line if you are the usual mostly uninformed ordinary citizen, is that you are locked into a system that really does not give you any really defendable rights. You are a victim and a slave to the system, whether you want to recognize that or not, and also whether you like it or not.

As I zoom forward toward finishing this book, and keep on finding new things that could be included, a few things mentioned in the remaining chapters will be revealing as well as somewhat bothersome to all of our readers.

Chapter 16

A REAL NEW YEAR'S DAY
& GOV'T FEARS E.T.'S

This is a very close copy of an article provided by Patrick H. Bellringer, editor in charge of the website **"fourwinds10.com"** which has been dedicated for a number of years toward providing the truth which is not being published in our regular media, and further providing revelations such as presented here.

Tuesday, August 17th. 2007 was day one of the cosmic year 2021. On that day we began the twenty first year since the Harmonic Convergence of August 17th. 1987. At that point in time, the great cycle of 206 million years of our Milky Way Galaxy (Orvonton Super Universe) turning around the Greatest Central Sun, returned to the zero point, and at that same time our Apsu Solar System in its orbit of 26,000 years around the Central Sun, Alcyone of the Pleiades, returned to its zero point, thus the harmonic convergence..

Our Gregorian calendar is off by nearly fourteen years for two main reasons. First, the Gregorian (Roman) calendar was based upon the birth date of Esu Emmanuel (Jesus Christ) as its beginning point. Thus, zero BC/AD was thought to be Esu's birthday, when in fact, his birth date was 8-8-8 BC by that calendar. Therefore, the calendar was off by eight years at its very beginning.

The other approximately six and one-half years of error is due to the miscalculations of the length of a given year over the period of 2,007 years. Leap year every fourth year, which gave the month of February a 29th day, was a crude way to "catch up" on the miscalculations.

The true calendar to coincide with true cosmic time should have had a thirteen month year of 28 days in each month, for a total of 364 days in each year. Each day of the week would have fallen on the same number each month. A calendar of 28 days per month would have corresponded with the 28 day cycle of the moon and with the 28 day menstrual cycle of the human female and certain other mammals.

The number 13 of the 13 months of the Cosmic Calendar is a heavenly number of great esteem, for it represents the number of the twelve disciples of Esu Emmanuel plus himself, making thirteen truth bringers, who brought truth to Earth some 2,000 years ago. They were the nucleus from which some truth has come down to us today over the stepping stones of time.

In this twenty-first year of the new great cycle (number 22) Earth Shan (planet of difficulty & sadness) is destined to be cleansed of all pollution and evil, and begin her recovery to her original pristine condition. For her to accomplish this, heaven has determined that all her people must be evacuated to safety via the starships of our Star Friends, who have come at this time, as the Hosts of Heaven for that purpose.

So, this New Year of Cosmic 2021 is destined to begin the most eventful year in the entire nearly four and one-half billion years of the life of our beloved planet. Is it not a great miracle that we are here at this very time to experience such a cosmic event--the birthing of a planet into fifth dimension? May you enjoy the ride, and may you be one to graduate into the fifth dimension along with our mother Earth.

E.T.'s, Secret Gov., Military, Oaths of Secrecy :
The only open and truthful newspapers, containing anything but propaganda, half-truths, outright lies and meaningless childish drivel, appear almost exclusively on the internet. There is an interesting one in Canada, called **"The Canadian National Newspaper"**, and on August 22nd. 2007, it contained a very interesting article by Paul Chen, Titled: **"Former U.S. military commander says elites hide from humanity knowledge and contact with many**

extraterrestrial civilizations"

Command Sergeant Major Robert Dean worked at NATO's Supreme Headquarters from 1963 - 1967, and during this time was stationed in the Operations Center with a Cosmic Top Secret clearance. "He claims to have viewed a secret NATO study that was commissioned to analyze the threat posed by UFO's to NATO operations in Eastern Europe." This was reported by Dr. Michael Salla, who is a scholarly researcher on extraterrestrial life and Earthbound human political implications, in the article entitled "Extraterrestrials Among Us", Exopolitics Journal, vol. 1:4 (October 2006): 284-300. The classified report was titled "An Assessment: An evaluation of a possible military threat to Allied Forces Europe". It focused on the dangers of UFO's being mistakenly identified as an incoming ballistic missile attack from the Soviet Union. Dean claimed that the NATO study identified four different extraterrestrial civilizations visiting Earth.

Dr. Salla stated that Commander Dean had said: "what really worried the NATO top brass was that some of the visitors looked so much like us that they were virtually undistinguishable, and that the NATO generals were paranoid over the possibility that some of the extraterrestrial visitors could be walking in the corridors of NATO or the Pentagon, or even the White House itself."

Dr. Salla further reports the following, in an interview documented by Bob Hieronimus, "Transcript of Interview with Bob Dean, March 24, 1996." Major Dean said further, that "here was a human group that looked so much like us that that really drove the admirals and the generals crazy because they determined that these people, and they had seen them repeatedly, they had had contact with them... These people looked so much like us they could sit next to you on a plane or in a restaurant and you'd never know the difference. Being military, and being primarily paranoid, that bothered the generals and admirals a little bit. That these intelligent entities could be involved with us, walking up and down the corridors of SHAPE (Supreme Headquarters Allied Powers Europe), walking down the corridors of the Pentagon. My God, it even dawned on a couple of them that these guys could even be in the White House! Of course, as I said, being paranoid in those years it really shook things up a little bit."

Dean also reported that government insiders feel that we are dealing with hundreds of ET civilizations, some intergalactic, some inter-dimensional. He noted that over 10 years ago, NASA set up a scientific committee, which came to the conclusion that there are an estimated 10 billion planets with intelligent life.

The article covers a lot more ground than I have covered here. However, I have now given you enough of its main points to perhaps start you toward a new perspective with regard to our extraterrestrial friends out there.

Chapter 17

HUMANOID IMMIGRANTS TO EARTH?

I am now going to provide you with some of the main parts of an article by Dr. Richard Boylan, Ph.D., COE. He had posted an article on his popular website, www.drboylan.com, concerning the subject. I think Dr. Boylan's website is the best in existence for the amount of information he provides concerning extraterrestrials, suppression of related information, the controlling Cabal, and a number of other connected things.

He recently posted his subject article, entitled: **Earth's First Step in Joining The Cosmic Family Is to Have Some of The Cosmic Family Join Us.**

I will quote directly from the first couple of paragraphs to fill you in on the basics, and then provide a summary of the balance of the article:

"Yesterday I sent out to my e-groups members an announcement that there was a group of Star Visitors who wished to find a home among us on Earth because their current world will not be suitable for habitation much longer. Given the urgency of the matter, I included in that e-mailing a request for a vote on whether the general people (as distinct from Cabal controlled governments) would welcome such a star group seeking to immigrate here. The voting group was a representative sample of humans who met the requisite criteria: a global-based population who are informed about star visitor matters, and who are not operating from the abundant disinformation and hostile propaganda so prevalent on the Internet and elsewhere. The representative human convenience sample selected were the 4,314 members of the UFO Facts, Dr Richard Boylan Reports and Starkids Hangout on line groups.

While some votes may still trickle in before Thursday is over, the vote outcome is so heavily weighted towards "yes" that it is beyond statistical probability that the outcome would change. The vote outcome? "Yes" = 92.2%, "No" = 0.04%, "Undecided" = 7.3%. Arguably, this is an overwhelming mandate. "- End of quoting.

Star Nations had decided not to send the entire race (3-½ million persons) to Earth. However, a carefully chosen group of 12 highly educated representatives of that humanoid race would be sent here to assist us primarily, to clean up radiation and other forms of pollution on our beautiful planet. Two Zeta Reticulans would come along with those folks as guardian/observers.

That peaceful and highly intelligent race of humanoids will be coming from a planet orbiting a red dwarf star in the Barnard's Star immediate neighbourhood of fellow red dwarf stars. They are a hybrid species that have lungs and systems that make them able to come to Earth without atmosphere or gravity adaption, except that our sun is brighter and they do need protection from that, and will spend much time indoors or end up being more active during evening and night hours.

There is a great deal more to Dr. Boylan's article, and you would be well advised to access his most interesting website and bring yourself up to date on this particular subject and numerous others. This would include a complete update on anti-gravity craft that the Cabal's secret government has been building since the 1960's.

Chapter 18

UNIFIED FIELD THEORY & EQUATIONS SUPPRESSED GOES BACK 150 YEARS+

There is an exceptionally honest, highly prolific and very scientific source of information in the spirit world, being a group soul referred to as Kryon, which has dictated a number of very informative books. Peter Farley, with Sue Ann Mikrut provided the following information, much of which was quoted by Kryon. Apparently this information is also now included in a 9-volume series providing the history of The New World Order, including their all-encompassing and exceptionally detailed plan for total enslavement of the human race.

Their website, as quoted at the bottom of their article of Jan 27th. 2008 as presented on www.fourwinds10.com , is www.4truthseekers.org   Obviously, they have tackled one of the most mysterious, secret and elaborate long term plans (conspiracies) ever imposed on the human race, and that series of books will be one of the greatest and most elaborate revelations in the last 100 years. Whether worded the same or not, this Unified Field information as presented here below, is directly from their above mentioned article. Although I am mostly familiar with the new realities of physics discussed therein, I could not explain any of it more clearly.

How does one make a time machine? Kryon here helps explain the basics of how this works, and some of the associated phenomena relating to spacecraft and how they travel, both through space as well as through time.

Density is the key to actual measured mass. Most of the Universe is made of elements that support simple size/density ratios. It's when scientists find the objects that don't behave this certain way that they are mystified. Remember this: Your observations are restricted to your own time frame.

Magnetics and electricity play a critical part in the

determination of the real attributes of mass, and the magnetic variables that determine the mass product, are often working within very small particles to create the density of an object and also its time frame! It is the small particle mechanics which actually determine the mass attributes of an object and therefore the gravity and time frame surrounding the object. (Thus the microcosm truly does create the macrocosm, just as the individual cells of our body make up the body as a whole, and also the time frame in which it exists). Can you imagine an object with zero density - no matter what the size? Very little in the Universe exists in this condition, but it can be artificially created, simply by using the density mechanics of what determines an object's actual mass. While you are pondering it, also consider negative mass, negative energy, and gravity that is reversed!

Experimenting with a magnetic field's lines of influence running at right angles to another electric field will bring you gratification in your search to alter the mass of an object. These are the mechanics to actually temporarily change small particle polarity behaviour, which translates to density, the lack of it, or its reverse (negative density). Be cautious, for you will also be creating a small time displacement, which can be dangerous to you physically until you understand how objects in altered time displacements correctly interact (one of the difficulties associated with the Philadelphia Experiment).

Do not make any assumptions about the shape of the interacting magnetic and electric fields, or what the medium should be to carry the polarity properties in such a system. Remember, however, that gas and liquid metals can also be used effectively to carry a charge. Do not be surprised if water under pressure also plays an important part in this system.

A true massless object no longer obeys the laws of your time frame physics. Wild starts and stops, speed and turns are well within the realm of a massless object, since it creates its own energy influence. Because of the very slight time displacement, it tends to change the number of electrons within the atoms directly in contact with it. This is a clue on how to detect a massless object, even if you can't see it. This should also now explain the magnetic anomalies around the UFO experiences that you have documented (many UFO's on film appear blurry or fuzzy because of this associated time differential between the UFO and other things around it in our time).

Gravitational anomalies of earth can create havoc with a system such as this, and this is why sometimes the vehicles crash (such as in Roswell after the nuclear testing had upset the earth's magnetic grid system in that area).

Much of the technical advancement in this field will be to apply very high and low density attributes to smaller and smaller amounts of matter, and it is the understanding of small particle polarity and behaviour that is the key to all of this.

One of the best sources on the cover-up of scientific knowledge is the Suppression of Vital Data in Physics by Byron Weeks. Weeks describes how the public is continually manipulated and our evolution and progress substantially restricted by the suppression, destruction, and/or alteration of significant, important information.

He refers in particular to an alteration of Maxwell's equations which resulted from Maxwell's extensive research into electro-magnetism. These alterations drastically affected the entire course of "mainstream" science and physics forever afterward, notably in the information made available to scientists and physicists of the time such as Einstein, as well as the subsequent conceptual framework which Einstein arrived at. To cut to the chase, the missing link which would provide the key to the Unified Field

Theory was deliberately cut out of Maxwell's equations by a rather sinister group of scientists before Maxwell's work was presented to the scientific community and the world. Of course, his original work and all the implications thereof are now known to the covert world government, as are the resultant advanced sciences and applications of this knowledge to very high technology.

This technology is being implemented in the furtherance of unquestionably dark agendas and goals related to the Great Plan itself, with consequences which are most certainly destructive to nearly every significant aspect of human life here on the planet, and even beyond. In Val Valerian's view, this is, in part, due to "...a general state of mind which has no understanding of, respect for, and connection with nature and the earth with its multitude of life forms. It is a state of mind which is the product of our current dehumanized, mechanistic and massively mind controlled (through every available means) existence, at the hands of the worldwide covert government and its super hi-tech arsenal of mind manipulating technologies.

For those whom are at all aware of it, the work of Wilhelm Reich simply hints at the wealth of unshared information about the free energy available to all of us, especially with regard to what he called "Orgone" energy, - some characteristics of which are electromagnetic in nature, but outside of the commonly understood "EM" frame of reference. Both Weeks' work and valerian's observations confirm what Kryon has suggested and make it obvious that anti-gravity machines and time machines are very probable if not definitely possible. From Week's book: "For thousands of years , many discoveries have been suppressed from the populations of the planet in order to keep them in bondage. The burning of the libraries of Alexandria is one example of how information can be suppressed. Another example would be the common technique of suppression of scientific information by alteration of the information itself."

Perhaps the most blatant and far reaching alteration of data was the alteration of Maxwell's equations. James Clerk

Maxwell was a mathematical genius who lived in the late 19th. century. His original work, which is available to covert scientific departments in the government, had the potential to radically alter the entire course of civilization.

Once all of the technical studies and accomplishments of Wilhelm Reich were fully in the hands of, and had been further confirmed by experimentation, by and on behalf of the secret government, Reich was jailed on some pretext, and eventually died (was assassinated?) in jail. The same situation applies to the work and discoveries of Viktor Shauberger, and Shauberger's achievements had great significance in new scientific areas, leading to new technologies, as eventually further developed and perfected toward the nefarious objectives of the "secret government".

"It is certainly clear to most of you by now that the human population can be easily manipulated by electronic means using various methods developed through the military industrial complex. What may not be clear to you is that many of the EM effects can be initiated from outside of what is normally seen as the electromagnetic spectrum. Just as a magnetic field in a wire is at right angles to the current flow, other fields and wave-forms exist that are an integral part of the electromagnetic spectrum, yet exist at a certain number of right angle rotations (orthogonal rotations) away from the electro-magnetic field components we are normally accustomed to. If these hyper-spatial components, which are not subject to the usual electromagnetic constraints of time and space, are generated and manipulated, they can in turn, generate EM effects that have the capability to influence human biology and consciousness."

Weeks goes on to take a brief look at how and by whom the equations of Maxwell were changed "in order to make subsequent open scientific development that would have influenced civilization in a positive way, impossible."

The following section by Vladimir Valerian, from his book,

"Matrix III", Volume One, contains further information about the massive deception and manipulation of scientific concepts which so extensively impacts our view of "reality' in this present day materialistic culture.

"In late 1864, James Clerk Maxwell published his epic material on electromagnetic waves. His material dealt not only with the electrical and magnetic waves, but also the relativistic/ethereal psychoactive component of these waves (representing electromagnetics of the second order and above). The equations also included transformations that enabled the change from inertial frames of reference to non-inertial frames of reference. Maxwell's original equations were written in Quatermion notation, a complex mathematical system available at that time, before vector analysis was introduced by Oliver Heaviside. Today's generalized equivalent of Quatermions is Tensors.

"In short, Maxwell's original work gave the necessary information for gravitational propulsion and psychoactive devices. Someone somewhere recognized this, for shortly after his death, the mathematician Oliver Heaviside, the chemist Willard Gibbs, and physicist Heinrich Hertz decided to "edit" or "interpret" Maxwell's famous equations or scalar components of Maxwell's original equations, because they represented potentials and not fields. Hertz thought potentials were akin to "mysticism", because "everybody knows" that fields contain mass, and mass cannot be created from apparently nothing, which is what potentials are, both literally and mathematically; they are an accumulation or reservoir of energy. Furthermore, not only did they throw away the gravitational component with the Quatermion/Scalar, but also postulated that gravitation and electro- magnetisms were mutually exclusive, not interdependent. That was the death blow to subsequent efforts by scientists to realize a functioning Unified Field Theory. Because of this one act, electromagnetism was reduced from its original five dimensions to only four: X,Y,Z and time. The element G was removed.

"Because of this deliberate act, twenty-two other errors exist today in electromagnetic theory. The very concepts of force, mass and charge are ill-defined, and the so-called "static" electrical charge has been discovered by Quantum mechanics not to be static at all, but to move rotationally by virtue of the Quantum mechanical spin. Finally, adding insult to injury, the so-called "imaginary components" of Maxwell's original equations as well as the mutilated version of the equations have also been discarded or ignored. With this last error, the door to hyper-spatial domains was forever closed, for the present mathematics and physics of electromagnetic theory do not allow for hyper-spatial domains (domains outside of three dimensions), supraliminal signals (signals that exceed the speed of light, or are infinite in speed), and a Unified Field Theory.

"The edited version of Maxwell's work, which every physicist and engineer has had to contend with, discards electro-gravitation, and avoids the unification of gravitation and electromagnetics. It also prevents the direct engineering of gravitation, space-time, time flow rates, free energy devices, and quantum changes, which is viewed by the altered equations that are vector-based as only a statistical change. The quartermion approach captures the ability to utilize electromagnetics and produce local curvature of space-time. Heaviside wrote a subset of Maxwell's equations where this capability is excluded.

"Dr. Henry Monteith has independently discovered that Maxwell's original Quatermion theory was a **Unified Field Theory**. Einstein assumed, because he only had access to the altered equations, that curving space-time could only be achieved by the weak gravitational force due to mass, that the local frame would always be a Lorenz frame, which would mean that all operations would be constrained to "conservation laws of physics".

"In the 1960's the Hertz replaced Cycles per Second. Since then, everyone thinks that all electromagnetic waves are Hertzian. Only the upper portion of the spectrum before infrared contains Hertzian waves. ELF and ULF are not. Waves in bio-systems and natural phenomena are not Hertzian in nature."

For what it's worth, I will suggest that this Hertz situation is every bit as deliberate toward confusing the rest of us, as the change from the Imperial twelve system to the metric ten system, when dealing with spatial matters. The base mathematics of the universe itself appears to fit with a twelve system. That has been understood by a few people since before 1960. Why should that change have been made, except to create more ignorance and confusion?

At the end of the article on www.fourwinds10.com by Peter Farley, with Sue Ann Mikrut, certain concerns were expressed, and follow up statements made, and those should also be expressed here, as they obviously related to why the article was posted on the four winds website. (Quoting)

"Why do we continue to tolerate this manipulation and control over every aspect of our lives? Why do the media and the school system (who are) supposed to educate and inform us, people who are supposed to debate these ideas, surrender to their suppression? It is because we have lost our true history, and because of the grooves and patterns that have been dug in our minds and those of our forebears for untold millennia. It is simple, as Christof says in the Truman Show when asked why Truman doesn't 'wake up' to his situation of his controlled matrix, he replies, and "We accept the reality of the world as presented."

Those of us who have chosen to live at this time are the forerunners of almost a new species. It is human, yet we are or will be at the same time actually manifesting heaven on Earth. We are receiving extra help from the masters and extraterrestrials, angelic beings, and learning to go more inward for our answers because we are so used to the lies and propaganda when seeking outside ourselves. The more we are able to go in and listen to that still quiet voice within us, the more we will be in tune with the changes that are occurring around us, and free of this Great Plan of ultimate control. As one writer puts it, " These INUTTERABLE CRIMES have been committed in the ludicrous notion that MAN HAS DOMINION OVER ANYTHING . . . So I ran the gamut of feelings from sad to mad to sobs of pure pain." Back to my own comments, relative to things said about the Freemasons in the closing part of the article, the scope of the plans of the Illuminati is already evident.

Our readers need to understand the long term nature and continuing evolution of those plans, to realize just how self-serving, cold-blooded and absolutely inhuman they have been, and continue to be.

In 1889, General Albert S. Pike, of the U.S. occupied the positions of Grand Master of the Central Directory of Washington D.C. (the head of D.C. Masonry), Grand Commander of the Supreme Council of Charleston (Head of American Masonry), and Sovereign Pontiff of Universal Freemasonry (Head of World Masonry). There is a letter which remains in the archives in London, England, between Albert Pike, and the head of European Freemasonry, and that letter was written in 1897, or a bit sooner, and it laid out certain long term objectives of the Freemasons.

In that letter, Pike stated that World War 1 was to begin in 1914, and that World War 2 was to begin in 1939, and that World War 3 was to begin between the 1980's and 2000, toward final establishment of the Luciferian New World Order. In that same letter he stated that "The Masonic religion should be, by all of us initiates of the high degrees, maintained in the purity of the Luciferian doctrine."

Chapter 19

TIME MACHINES, UNDERGROUND BASES
& HUMAN CLONES

Time Machines:
This one might stretch your "credibility gap" or "window of believability" quite a bit. In my ball park, the existence of Time Machines since prior to the end of World War II has been known for a long time. The ideas and technology for both time machines and anti-gravity craft were introduced to the Germans by extra-terrestrials from the Pleiades in the late 1930's - probably 1937. The Americans had a similar opportunity to gain from cooperation with those folks, but joined up with a more negative group from Orion, referred to as "the greys". It looks like the Germans gained much, and the Americans stayed behind for quite a while.

The Montauk Project was begun at the behest of the Nazis, at an "abandoned" air base on Montauk Point, Long Island, New York, before World War 2 was over. (The deeper truth from an earlier point in time is that the British trained Hitler, and the Nazis were financed by the Americans, and the Montauk project later financed by the Nazis).

Don't ask me to elaborate on that one here, as it would add a lot more pages than necessary. I could also digress laterally on a couple of dozen other bothersome subjects as brought up in this book. Now, let's get on with the story, whether it seems believable or not.

The Philadelphia Experiment was followed by the Montauk Project. The Philadelphia Experiment was originally an American project, while Montauk was a follow-through on an earlier German project. Don't get confused here, as the illuminati parasites in the U.S., Britain & Germany were secretly running the show, and told you less than nothing...

The fact that Americans and Germans were killing each other

in the meantime, did not matter a damn to those folks. They were running the American and British and German governments at the same time. Don't lose sight of the fact that the overall objective was the One World Order, and total enslavement of the entire population of this planet. Remember that General Pike, the Grand Master, laid out the plan to the Freemasons prior to 1900, including World Wars 1,2 & 3.

Time machine technology possessed by the Third Reich in 1943, was improved to a fine state of the art, from 1945 to 1986, as the first objective of the Montauk Project. They managed to demonstrate that they could go back in time as far as 260,000 years. In a more bothersome sense, they went forward in time more than 9000 years. However, in the material I read on the subject, "The Montauk Project" by Al Bielek and Preston Nichols, and since corroborated by others familiar with Unified Field physics, there is a problem. Time moves forward as we might observe from our "now" perspective, as evolving probabilities. The Unified Field Theory suggests random probabilities, related to sub-atomic particles.

Another point to ponder concerning the nature of time, is that it was discovered early on in the series of Montauk Project experiments, that time is cyclical here, in the third dimension, on this planet. It runs in 20 year cycles, with 10 year sub-cycles, and those 20 and 10 year cycles tie back to our 20 year sunspot cycle. This situation apparently has to be worked into any system of proposed time cycle control of events as might be applied to the methodology described below.

As a consequence of the nature of time as experientially determined, those folks learned that the certainty of an event in the future cannot exist, unless a probability pathway is created. The consequentially intervening events are being progressively created and varied as to its evolution, as we move forward. We can be quite certain a few days ahead, if the issue involved is powerfully imprinted on the minds of enough of the participants and onlookers.

These findings indicated to those nefarious parasites that a progressive series of adjustments had to be made from one point in time, where the idea is inserted, to another point in time when it is supposed to become the new reality. If all this stuff bothers you, and you are not bound up with religion, or egotistical enough to assume there is no creator, you might acknowledge that God and scientific realities do co-exist, whether "religion" acknowledges that or not.

Anyway, a bothersome truth becomes apparent, as most of us thinkers end up digging deep enough into the meaning of things. I arrived there a while ago, and many of you who read this material may have done so, or surely might get there as you keep digging. There is a creator. There is a GOD over all of us, and that tiny bit of soul material in each of us is only a tiny particle of our creator, and interacts with everything.

What eventually becomes apparent, is that what each of us thinks, severally and collectively creates our future within the solidity of our present world. That also now confirms those things I have chased down over the years, such as the fact that this is a completely interacting holographic universe, which is indeed a continuously evolving, expanding all encompassing thought form of our creator.

Why do the parasites have to keep chiselling away with their time machines to create their own absolutely solid future? Go a bit backward and review what I have just said. They know about the world of spirit, which is the world of light, and to succeed they must deal with it the way it works, whether they like it or not. This is a free will planet in a free will universe, but in spite of that, those parasites (the Satanists or Luciferians) will proceed until they get stopped in their tracks.

What has our criminal Illuminati "elite" (parasite) leadership been doing with this technology in the meantime, as they govern the most militarily powerful and fearsome nation on the face of the planet? If you back up a bit, you will note that time in our situation runs in 20-year cycles, and 10 year sub-cycles. It then seems too coincidental that many major events related to the actions of our present rulers have occurred on years ending in 3, such as the Federal Reserve having been placed in criminal control of the U.S. money system in 1913, and other major changes or legislation in their favour, have been occurring at every 10 year increment since that time.

Let's bear in mind that with the use of the time machine, 1913, could have been accessed at any 10 year incrementally later point in time, up to and including 2003. The Philadelphia Experiment took place in 1943, and was later accessed and set straight in 1983, at Montauk, and that was the first correcting exercise. Don't think for a minute that 1913 could not have also been accessed to make subtle changes in what was going on then. Those Illuminati parasites have been exceptionally busy with mind control of the masses by the media in the meantime, while trying to guarantee their ultimate long term success with leadership of the U.S., or stopping anyone else of better intentions.

The illuminati have been trying to tailor events and consequences to serve their own agendas, since the late 1930's. Some idiot said a long time ago," what you don't know can't hurt you." In light of the many nefarious things being done by the Luciferian parasites to ensure our enslavement, that doesn't wash at all.

It is surely more than a bit bothersome that those parasites are in control at this time to such a complete extent. However, as time progresses, there are greater numbers of us who already know what is really going on, and rather soon, those absolutely immoral Luciferians are going to face the music big time. We should all look forward to that taking place in 2008.

Underground Cities & Military Bases:

I am aware that at least 131 underground establishments exist beneath the U.S. alone. More recently, I have read that there are more than 1,500. There are also others in Canada and England. A person that I am aware of, by the name of Serge Monast, a French Canadian investigative reporter, had reported something like 129 of those in the U.S. before he was assassinated. I have read two of his personally produced and sirlox bound books with maps showing where those underground locations are. He also had maps showing the locations of a serious number of above ground concentration camps. I also have seen a VCR presentation by a geologist who spent many years working underground on the construction of those bases and interconnecting tunnels. He also ended up being eventually assassinated by the CIA, and was found dead, with a wire wrapped around his neck.

This was after numerous earlier attempts to assassinate him had failed. His name was Phil Schneider.

A large number of those secret government underground locations are interconnected by thousands of miles of tunnels, and are served by a very modern high speed underground railway system. Many of those underground facilities are D.U.M.B.'s (Deep Underground Military Bases).

One other odd thing that I learned is that there are more than 16 underground levels below Area 51, and its lowest level 16 is connected by rapid transit to the inner earth civilization, referred to as Agartha. The person, who described that situation, concerning Area 51, was a military type who had remained and worked underground at the base for 11 years.

The main underground human cloning operation in the U.S. is at Camp David. That is where U.S. presidents and many others have been cloned for many years. There are underground mind control and conditioning centres in California which were being run by the illuminati during "Project Monarch", which trained mind controlled subjects for everything from prostitution, to espionage, (or both), as well as being suicide bombers and assassins.

Remember the Manchurian Candidate? The same thing was happening real time, with others being similarly trained at underground locations in the U.S. = (Project Monarch)

One of the largest examples in the U.S. is the deep underground facility under the Denver International Airport. It is of further interest to note that in the main public area inside that airport are murals consisting of completely Luciferian subject material. I have also read in limited published materials that there are also underground maximum security prison facilities, and a couple of very elaborate underground gas chambers and crematorium facilities, far more elaborate than anything put together by the Germans during World War Two.

Ref: http//www.fourwinds10.com & http//www.rense.com
and The Phoenix Journals - available on fourwinds10.com - Also, VCR's by Phil Schneider would shake your boots, but they may be hard to find.

Cloning of Humans Began by 1970:
Getting back to quietly hidden, but nevertheless obvious truths, the Rockefeller banking and industrial family faction of the illuminati, was controlling the secret government situations in the U.S., including the CIA, NSA, FBI, MJ-12, and all of the secret under-ground laboratories and facilities. The same was probably true during the time frame up to the present, where the Rothschild financial and corporate empire, along secretly, with the "Royal Families" of Europe, quietly together, controlled similar things throughout Europe, (including Russia).

Based on a number of privately informative books and articles I have read in the meantime, concerning those two illuminati controlled financial and industrial empires, they were quietly and seriously competing with each other. With limitless greed and a morbid desire for absolute control of the people, each wanted to assure that they would get to the top of the pile. They were then looking at the future time when the illuminati would finally succeed at enslaving the entire world population according to their long term Master Plan.

The most currently shocking example of the extent of cloning, how long it has been going in, and where it is being most effectively applied, try this one on for size... As of November 2007, the President Bush of the U.S. that we are most commonly familiar with, has had 47 replacement clones activated to keep the illusion going that he is still alive and functioning. Carter, Clinton and others have also been cloned as well, along with a sizeable percentage of folks running the U.S., including key members of congress, the senate, the military, and other important departments.

Ref: Whitebuffaloenterprises@yahoo.com (Master Lemlet) www.fourwinds10.com - Complete background on cloning at 3 process levels, by both the Rothschild and Rockefeller factions/groups, involving primarily the U.S. and Russia, going back to 1970 and earlier.

Chapter 20

DARK SIDE LOSING, PHYSICAL & SPIRITUAL CHANGES COMING - N.E.S.A.R.A. LAW KEPT SECRET, & NOW PROPERLY EXPLAINED

The Dark Side Is Losing & Being Exposed:
For anyone who has been consistently paying attention, when this is being written, there are so many areas where you could see what is happening. At this critical point in time, everything is coming to a head.

The key perpetrators of the One World Order, or New World Order, as it has also often been called, and those who have been feeding us the bullshit, are now being finally exposed, arrested, and forced to "face the music'. This largely unreported background action so far, has related primarily to the banking cabals, their now largely bankrupt banks, their toilet paper money, and the fact that that corrupt bunch and their minions are massively looting the system.

By February 15th. 2008, there were already more than 6000 of those thieves, scam artists and other experts related to fraud and embezzlement, who had been arrested, shipped off to Europe, and locked up. The reasons for shipping them off to Europe, are that their thievery was largely from the Europeans, and also, once they were gone to Europe, the puppet (or cloned) U.S. president could not pardon them, which he might have done. Arrests had been done by the U.S. Provost Marshall, and later a special Marines unit.

All of that is ok., and essential to achieving a new situation where we no longer will be citizens of a Nazi dictatorship, ("The Fourth Reich") which has been slowly, quietly and gently put into place, with much tighter laws than Hitler ever had) while we were not paying attention. In this case, if the truth hurts, aspirins will not provide relief. Mushrooms thrive with adequate doses of bullshit. If you seriously delve into what has really been going on for the past 30 years or so, the successful application of carefully planned and gently sequenced mega doses of bullshit will become rather apparent.

Now, early in 2008, a lot of formerly placid mushrooms have begun to pay attention, learn a bit, and recognize some of what is going on.

Physical & Spiritual Changes Will Affect All of Us:

Planet Earth and all of its occupants are about to experience an upward shift in frequency, from the third to the fifth dimension. The fifth dimension is the equivalent to us in the physical solidity of our third dimensional world, as being totally a world of spirit, or heaven, as we might call it.

During our present life times, for each of us, we are to experience our Karma, (spiritual law of cause & effect) consequences, or forgive ourselves, and those to whom we have caused physical or spiritual discomfort. We are then to live the rest of our life, feeling and projecting honesty, goodness, fairness and love toward all others and the planet at large, if we are to move forward and upward to the fifth dimension. All of us are EQUAL fragments (souls) of the universal consciousness of our creator. Remember, "Do unto others"? - That's the deeper reason, in spite of anything our pious churches or dominating controllers might have to say...

Our planet is a magnificent living entity, and she will go through a period of violent upheavals in the process of healing herself. Those of us who have experienced, or have been forgiven from our remaining karma, will move forward with the planet when the dimensional shift takes place. In the more immediate future, shortly preceding the upcoming earth changes, three separate groupings of us humans will each be taken to a separate location by our extraterrestrial neighbours.

The illuminati, most of their minions, and all other folks of lower frequency and spiritual development, will be taken to a new planet in a new solar system, which is now experiencing its own Stone Age, with the usual large dinosaurs, and other Stone Age creatures. It has been said that the name of this very large planet is Herculobus. A sizeable number of our illuminati criminals etc., have already been taken there by now, in the month of February of 2008.

The next group, although not greatly spiritually developed, but nevertheless good people, just needing further development, will be taken on to another more highly evolved third dimensional planet. They will learn and experience their essential remaining lessons before moving onward and upward.

The remainder of us, who are more ready for ultimate ascension to the fifth dimension, will be temporarily removed from the surface of this planet, while she goes through her essential cleansing process, which will involve very violent changes to her entire surface, followed by a period of re-growth of her pristine forests, and regeneration of the remaining elements of nature. We will be trained and seriously assisted in the meantime to have our bodies' frequency rise to fifth dimensional frequency level. Then we will ascend with mother Earth into the new reality.

The dimensional shift is said to be now occurring throughout this entire universe, and is unavoidable, with an upward shift taking place at the time of one complete orbital rotation of this entire galaxy, which takes 206 million years.

Our Earth folks and extraterrestrial friends knew about this situation a very long time ago, as the minor cycles leading up to this major occurrence are mentioned in the ancient history books from India, referred to as the "Vedas".

I had said at the beginning of this book, that information directly dictated from the other side of this reality is usually far more consistently accurate than anything we are being spoon fed by our present totally controlled media. Here is a broader piece of information to add to what had been presented above, which was dictated by our ascended masters on February 9th. 2008:

"Our Planet is not the only one moving into the higher dimension after it is cleared from the illuminati, but all two million universes are also going into higher dimensions. Each universe has 12 constellations, each constellation has 12 galaxies, each galaxy has 12 solar systems, and each solar system has 12 planets.

We were programmed by the Dark Forces to believe that our Creator God was not capable of creating but one planet, called Earth..." You will note a couple of contradictions in terms in that presentation as given, and that sort of thing has been deliberately arranged as the dark side has changed and reversed such terms to seriously limit our perspectives. My own observation in this area, is that from the many thousands of pages of material I have read, as sourced from extraterrestrial folks, they have used virtually identical descriptions as to constellations, galaxies, and solar systems, as our Ascended Masters.

N.E.S.A.R.A. is in the works - What is it? and what will it mean to all of us?

Most of what is provided here on this subject is from fourwinds10.com...

NESARA stands for: **National Economic Security and Reformation Act.** In the U.S., most can remember Willie Nelson doing the Farm Aid concerts in order to help farmers save their farms. Willie Nelson began doing Farm Aid concerts to raise money for the farm families who were losing their farms during the 1970's and 1980's.

In the 1980's some U S farmers pursued actions that had been put into motion years earlier and sued U.S. bankers for having illegally foreclosed on their farm properties. These farmers, having done extensive research, realized that many of the farm foreclosures were due to illegal tricks by the U.S. bankers. The farmers' law suits uncovered collusion by corrupt U.S. government officials with the dishonest bankers. A whole array of farmer's lawsuits went through the state, Federal, and U.S. Supreme Court processes. The U.S. Supreme Court decisions found that the farmer's petitions were valid.

The Supreme Court validated the farmer's petitions for restitution from the U.S. Federal Government by awarding restitution to the farmers. Due to the massive government fraud, there was also a requirement that other Americans be given the opportunity to file for restitution of damages done by the Federal Government. These historic court decisions became the basis for the process by which the people in all 50 states of the United States submitted bank claims for restitution of damages by the Federal Government. We all owe these brave farmers, attorneys, and U.S. Supreme Court judges in the farm claims lawsuit's a huge debt of gratitude for having taken on the Federal Government and the bankers, thereby exposing their corruption and illegal tricks.

In addition to the awarding of financial damages, the U.S. Supreme Court found that the farmer's claims of Federal Government fraud were also true. The U.S. Supreme Court required that major government reforms be enacted at the same time as the payment of damages to the farm claims people. The U.S. Supreme Court's finding on the Farm Claims lawsuits of federal Government fraud are part of the legal foundations of NESARA. It was stipulated that all these landmark court decisions remain secret until the government and banking reforms were made public, and the Farm Claims restitution funds were ready to be paid.

In June 2000, a secret law (NESARA) previously passed in March, 2000, by the U.S. Congress came to the attention of some citizens. This law was passed constitutionally and included a gag order with the penalty of death, if any official involved publicly discussed it prior to its official announcement.

In this same month, (June 2000) a White Knight (a military intelligence contact), said that this secret law:

1.) **Eliminated the IRS and Federal Income Taxes;**
2.) **Provided certain major debt forgiveness for people in the U.S.**
3.) **Would implement a new U.S. banking and monetary system, using precious metals based currency.**
4.) **Would absorb the Federal Reserve into the U.S. Treasury Department.**
5.) **Would restore our personal liberties, and implement mass improvements in the Federal Government, and much more.**

In mid-October, 2000, a White Knight high intelligence contact advised that the secret law had been signed by President Bill Clinton on October 10. 2000, and a few days later the acronym assigned to its name was NESARA. This stands for National Economic Security and Reformation Act. Because of the U.S. Supreme Court's requirement to keep the lawsuits secret, all official word of NESARA was forbidden until the corrections to the Federal Government, banking improvements, and prosperity programs distributions were ready to be implemented. (All the money deviously stolen from the American people by illegal and unconstitutional legislation, plus coercion with powerful politicians, civil servants and government at large is to a serious extent about to be repaid to the American people through the NESARA legislation.) The "prosperity programs" will come up later, and relate directly to this situation.

The prevailing gag order is why the first official word on NESARA is to be the pending public announcement to all humankind. The reason why all humankind will be informed and involved in NESARA and other foreign based versions of its benevolent actions and consequences is that the same bankers controlling the U.S. system have done much the same things to the banking systems and citizens in virtually all of the other countries in the world.

The interrelated move by all countries and all banks to a world wide new precious metals based monetary system is essential firstly, to keep useless and valueless fiat currency out of our world monetary systems, and secondly to establish a single stable base system of value which would necessarily apply to all of our world monetary systems. For instance, there will be no more of the disparities such as $30.00 per hour in Canada for a plumber or carpenter, and 50 cents to $3.00 per hour for the same work in any so-called under developed country. The same will apply to all manufacturing jobs etc., and The U.S., Canada and others of the more developed countries will not have their people unemployed and going broke while the elite and corporate controllers are becoming progressively wealthier on the backs of slave labour in other countries.

The White Knights required the U.S. Government to agree to distribute all these long-awaited prosperity programs at the same time as the implementation of the new banking and government improvements. Legally binding accords were signed by various heads of the Federal Government over the last few years that set forth the conditions of how all this would occur, and which guaranteed the funding of the prosperity programs. These accords are the legally bonding instruments used to put in place these momentous banking, government and prosperity activities.

Those opposed to this in banking, government, military and the legal world have used every trick possible along the way to delay the completion of the thousands of steps involved in aligning all these programs, the world-wide banking and monetary improvements and the U.S. Government reforms. They know that their power and control ends with the implementation of all the requirements in the NESARA law. This why the opposition ordered the World Trade Centre, Pentagon, and Pennsylvania attacks on September 11, 2001.

They knew that the final word had been given to notify the networks to get ready to broadcast the NESARA announcement.

We are entering a new era of peace, prosperity, harmony and vitality on Planet Earth Shan. Unfortunately, in order for everything to be executed successfully, much had to be kept secret in order for these great improvements to be made ready. Now is the time for this all to take place and complete the plans that our brave American reformers laid down fifty years ago.

Ref: For more information go to www.fourwinds10.com

Chapter 21

CANADA'S INCOME TAX -
LEGISLATION, PRACTICE & "LEGALITY"?

As we go forward from here, many Americans have heard that their income tax system of things is probably illegal and there have been cases where it could not stand up in court. You might find the Canadian situation interesting ....

Here are excerpts from a paper that was delivered in October 1991, by Mr. Murray Gauvreau, of Alberta, at a seminar of the Canadian League of Rights, in Calgary, which was published in the July, 1992 issue of the "Canadian Intelligence Service" (55 - 8th. Ave. S.E., High River, Alberta T1V 1E8).

As a result of having taken advantage of the many career advancement courses offered by the Life Insurance Industry, I became aware that the banks have the exclusive right to issue currency in Canada, as determined by the Federal Bank Act. But I didn't see them printing money, so I decided to find out exactly how they do issue currency. My search led me back into the early history of our nation, and into the history of our Province.

1867 - The B.N.A. Act:
So let's go back a ways, to the year 1867, and look into the pages of the Canadian Constitution, commonly known as the British North America (B.N.A.) Act. Therein lies the real solution to the ailments, both social and economic, that our country suffers from today. It is the same document today that it was when it was written so long ago.

The B.N.A. Act was written in order to establish the legal basis for this country. All laws enacted in Canada, whether by municipal, provincial or federal government, must comply with the terms of the B.N.A. Act. If they do not, they are then unconstitutional. Or in legal terms "ultra vires." and can be disallowed as law. The document belongs to the people of

Canada, and not to the parliamentarians or the courts, or to the Prime Minister and the Premiers.

The Canadian Constitution was not changed or altered when it was brought home by Mr. Trudeau, as some suggest. However, there was a very important addition made to it at that time. That addition was the Canadian Bill of Human Rights. Today the Canadian Constitution, as we know it, is comprised of the original B.N.A. Act, and the Human Rights Act, together.

Direct Taxation Belongs To Provinces:
There are two specific sections of the B.N.A. Act that deal with the delegation of authority between the Federal and Provincial Governments. Sections 91 and 92 deal with authority for various types of taxation, who has authority to levy which taxes, and various other areas of jurisdiction. **The act is very specific in its direction. The right to tax income, known as "direct" tax, was delegated to the provinces; and it was clearly indicated that any monies so raised must be raised provincially, and used for provincial purposes.**

The Federal Government was denied the right to levy income tax. But the Supreme Court of Canada goes further. It states that no level of government is allowed to transfer its authority to another level of government, and if transfer were attempted by one level, it could not legally be accepted by another.

On October 3, 1950, the Supreme Court of Canada handed down a decision in the case involving the Lord Nelson Hotel in Halifax, Nova Scotia, against the Attorneys-General of Nova Scotia and Canada. The case involved the transfer of powers from the Provincial to the Federal Government, and was directly related to the Income Tax Act. In a seven-judge unanimous decision, the highest court in our land ruled that power transfers cannot legally take place. The Federal Government was

given until 1962 to remove itself from all such power-transfer agreements, including the income tax business, and to scrap the Income Tax Act.

Clearly, the Federal Government has no constitutional right to engage in the income tax business, or any other type of direct taxation, whether on behalf of itself or on behalf of the provinces. Therefore, the Income Tax Act is, in itself, unconstitutional, and need not to be obeyed.

The Federal Government can create its own currency:
It is interesting to note that the same sections of the B.N.A. Act that disallow the Federal Government the right to collect income tax, did however provide for a means whereby the Federal Government could raise capital. Sections 91 (14,15,16,28, 29 and 20) give the Federal Government the authority and the responsibility, for the control and issue of our currency, based upon the resources and wealth of the nation. They were given an unlimited supply of debt-free money with which to operate the country. All they had to do was print it. And they did just that for the first 46 years of our country.

Government gives banks credit monopoly:
Then, some 46 years after confederation, in 1913, our parliamentarians were poorly advised in committing a grave injustice to future generations of Canadians by passing an amendment to the B.N.A. Act (without referendum) commonly known as the Bank Act.

By this act, the Federal Government gave to the private banks the sole right to create the financial credit (the "money") of our nation.

And for the last 79 years, the private banking system has been exercising this monopolistic prerogative of creating and controlling the Canadian people's financial credit.

Well, banks don't work for free. They charge "interest". They even charge interest to the Government. And interest can never be repaid; it just keeps adding up, and up, and up, until today our national debt alone is approaching 600 billion.

Banks do not lend out depositors' money:
Does anybody here know where the banks get the money that they lend out? Actually, most people assume that they lend out depositors' money, but the Bank Act specifies that the bank must retain the depositors' money on account, and must pay him interest on it.

So, where else might the bank get the money?
The Bank Act also specifies that the bank may create, out of nothing, new credit ("money") through loans. But that it must have a relationship to the deposits. Originally, the banks were allowed to lend out six times their deposits, but today banks are allowed to issue new credit up to 26 times their deposits. That means that if I deposit my $1,000 in a Canadian bank. Then that bank can issue loans to the tune of $26,000. Go to the bank, get a loan, and ask for the loan proceeds in cash. No matter the size of the loan, you cannot get it in cash - it must be deposited to you account, and cheques written in order to access the money. No tangible money is ever created; only debits and credits (figures) are created.

Today in Canada, the only source of money, whether for private, corporate, or governmental needs, is a loan from a bank. But you can never borrow your way out of debt. You can only borrow your way into bankruptcy, at which time you turn your back on your assets and your hard work, and give up possession of it to those to whom you owe money, but who gave absolutely no vested interest in your property.

1917: the Federal income tax:
Now that we understand that the national debt can never be fully repaid using the current system of finance, the question arises: How then, does it get paid? In 1917, after finding out that the debt was beginning to build, the Federal Government usurped the powers of the provincial governments and, under

the guise of the War Debt, they instituted the War Debt Income Tax Act which was unconstitutional then, and it is still unconstitutional today. When it was enacted, it was on a voluntary basis, at a rate of 10%, and applied only to those earning $10,000 or more per year. In 1917, the average yearly salary was about $250.

The Income tax act could have more appropriately been named the Bank Interest Debt Income Tax Act; but then, people would have fought to the death to keep it out of effect. Since that time, the Federal Government has seen fit to increase the tax rate as high as 65% of high income individuals, and has also seen fit to remove or lower limits to the point that, as you know, everyone is required to pay...

And now we have had the GST, which in my opinion is equally as unconstitutional, rammed down our throats by a group of Mp's that brashly and boldly declare that they are smarter than we are, and they know best...

Facing up to reality:
Our Federal Government has gone so far away from the Constitution, in nearly every area of jurisdiction that it now conspires to change it altogether. But that is not the solution. Getting back to the way it was written is the solution... Each one of us selects his mode and method of doing battles with oppressive government. Some of us do it by speaking out... some of us join non-party political groups. Some of us pray, and most of us do nothing. We have a condition called the "ostrich syndrome". If we ignore it and don't look at it, it might go away! But remember this: If your head is in the sand, your butt is an open target!

The Hart System: Tax Avoidance = Federal Income Tax is illegal:
I handle my fight personally using a system called the Hart System of Effective Tax Avoidance. Gerry Hart passed away recently in Winnipeg, but not before becoming Canada's undisputed champion No. 1 tax

fighter. Mr Hart for many years opted to take an aggressive and active position against oppressive government, and he has not paid income tax in nearly 50 years. During that time, he has been imposed upon, charged, harassed, his privacy invaded, and his person subjected to illegal search. But he has never given an inch. He has been to the Manitoba Court of Appeal 22 times, but has never lost.

In 1950, Gerry Hart received a copy of a Vancouver newspaper article which reported on a recent ruling made by the Supreme Court of Canada. He then requested a copy of the ruling itself, from the Supreme Court Chancery in Ottawa. He also requested a copy of the B.N.A. Act, because the ruling quoted various sections of that document. He found, just as the newspaper had reported, that Section 91 and 92 of the B.N.A. Act do not allow for the Federal Government to be in the Income Tax business.

The two documents - the Supreme Court ruling and the B.N.A. Act - have been the basis of his battle, and the only two documents he has needed. He has never had the benefit of legal counsel, and has chosen to appear in the court by himself. His only evidence has been those two documents. Charges against him have been thrown out of court 22 times. The last time, some twelve or so years ago, Revenue Canada was told that if it ever brought Gerry Hart back into court, Revenue Canada itself, would be charged with contempt of court.

Gerry Hart has never been convicted under the Income Tax Act. As he says, "Income tax is illegal. Therefore the collection of it is also illegal. Since Revenue Canada has no legal method of collecting income tax, they must resort to illegal means." Those illegal means include harassment, intimidation, illegal search, illegal seizure, violation of privacy, extortion, coercion, and complete ignorance and contempt for the human rights of Canadian citizens...

We have various books and booklets available to help educate on how to prepare to stop paying those illegal taxes. If our "Tax Kit" can help you to avoid several thousands of dollars of tax, it is certainly worth its small investment. Be sure to protect yourself from Revenue Canada before you get involved in the tax fight. Read the books and find out how...

If you still have questions after you have read the books, then call me. I'll try to help you. I have not paid income tax since 1978, and I have used Gerry Hart's system of Effective Tax Avoidance. I know it works, I am living proof.

Murray Gauvreau - www.prolognet.qc.ca/clyde/tax.htm

Further Closing Comments on this Income Tax situation:
In an article called "Thirst For Justice" the Canadian author of the article, Jean Pierre Richard, made the following bothersome comment: "In his 1993 report, Canada's Auditor General calculated that of the $423 billion in net accumulated debt from 1992, only $37 billion (8.75%) went on actual goods and services. All the rest (91%) consisted of interest charges. This should tell us how we have all become slaves."

American folks reading this could also make themselves aware that the deviousness of the passing of their legislation in 1913, and their own traitorous "elected?" government's sneaky actions with regard to the IRS situation was very similarly carried out, quietly, without public outcry at the time..

As any Americans or Canadians could suggest to themselves, it doesn't seem contradictory that one could be a mushroom and a sucker at the same time, as one has obviously led to the other. All of this, of course, has occurred with the total cooperation of the illuminati controlled media. There has been a great deal of brainwashing going on, and 95% of our citizens would probably be hard pressed to acknowledge that anything of that nature has taken place.

Chapter 22

SUGGESTED SOURCES OF UNBIASED
& TRUTHFUL INFORMATION

Observations:

It would usually be normal to lay out the books first. However, the newer reality in our present time frame would suggest otherwise. If we want to get up to date in a short length of time, without spending a serious amount of money on a few books, we should start with the internet.

Those of us who have been paying attention to the internet, and have sifted out most of the bullshit, are clearly aware that the current truth of things is there, and is reasonably easy to find. If you haven't dealt with the internet to any extent, speak to someone who has some practical experience before your fiddle around with it. Then make notes, so you don't waste your time.

A person who has serious experience at dealing with the internet will know how you can shortcut into almost any subject area you want to find. The next and even more important stage to deal with is how you can move backward toward earlier material to bring yourself more up to date on any subject.

Why do I say these things? Both books and the internet are simply ways of presenting information to the public. However, the internet remains independent.

The illuminati and their controlled suckers have been seriously trying to stop the internet, and haven't been able to slow it down, as the current generation uses it to keep themselves up to date. In the meantime, those younger folks have been letting each other know what our illuminati controllers have been legislating to reduce or curtail our personal freedoms, and to control us totally, with no potential for change, once their control is established.

A majority of those younger lads are no different from a majority of my much older generation. Most of them would like their routine unchanged, their football or hockey games to be close to #1, on their agenda. Their cold beer should also be available next to their favourite lazy boy chair in front of the idiot box or boob tube. If the media has not revealed something to this particular turkey, even if he is a university grad, he is either going to be a self-appointed expert saying it isn't so, or that he just isn't interested, and that's it.

The way I see it, probably a good 5% of those younger folks are going to be taking things more seriously. They are the real leaders, and will make waves one way or another, no matter what the totally controlled media has to say. In this book, I want their attention. This world has to be changed for the better, or at its present rate, it is not going to survive, and we humans are going to become extinct in the process.

The human race must no longer be controlled by a ridiculously small percentage of criminals who think they are superior or "the elite", and have some self-appointed right to that assumption. Among them, of course, are the banking families with their immeasurable fortunes, and another bunch of egotistical folks who control our corporations which in turn are presently controlling all of our governments.

Money, greed, egotism & the enslavement of the rest of the human race are at the top of the agenda for those who are presently at the top. They are almost to the point of being successful at the enslavement part. While most of us have been asleep, they have taken away virtually all of our individual and collective levels of freedom. The pertinent legislation has been passed in the U.S., Canada and the European Union at this point in time.

Books:

1.) **Behold A Pale Horse** - by: William Cooper - Light Technology Publishing, P.O. Box 1495, Sedona, AZ 86336 U.S., including the suppression of UFO's, assassination of James Forrestall, founding and operation of MJ-12, Eisenhower and extraterrestrials, dumping of President Nixon, membership with names, of the Council on Foreign Relations, the complete list of 24 Zionist protocols as originally laid out during the time of Napoleon, etc.

2.) **History of The One World Order** - said to be a 9 volume series. This can be checked out on the website : www.4truthseekers.org It is far too broad elaborate and complete to afford description here. It is like a complete University "Major" in terms of knowledge and education.

3.) **The 13th. Tribe** - The Khazarian Empire and Its Heritage, by Arthur Koestler.

4.) **Vatican Assassins** - by Eric Phelps

5.) **The International Jew** - The World's Foremost Problem - by Henry Ford

6.) **Lost Science** - by Gerry Vassilatos

7.) **You Are Becoming A Galactic Human-** by Sheldan Nidle & Virginia Essene

9.) **Your Galactic Neighbors** – by Sheldan Nidle

10.) **The Red Terror In Russia** - by Sergey Melgounov

11.) **The New Underworld Order** – by Christopher Story

12.) **The Biggest Secret** – by David Icke

Uncensored Websites:

1.)   www.fourwinds10.com brings out the real truth behind most significant events and happenings around the world, from economics to politics, and if you want to know what the dark side is doing, you are most likely to find out here, before the truth appears at other sources as further corroboration. etc..

2.)   www.rense.com has a very good percentage of things which would normally be kept out of our regular news media, and often is a good corroboration to what you can find on fourwinds10.

3.)   www.cloakanddagger.com this is a very private and seriously uncensored website. They charge $30.00 U.S. every 6 months for an active membership, with access to a private archives section which kicks hell out of the regular news media coverage of many things, political and economic, etc.

4.)   www.arcticbeacon.com this one also often tells you what the establishment and its totally controlled news media is unlikely to, or would never tell you. Etc. This is Greg Szymanski's website.

5.)   www.paoweb.com this is Sheldan Nidle's website. Along with references to the Galactic Federation, etc., and his books, tapes and discs, there are weekly reports by the Galactic Federation, dictated by their local representative nation, the Sirians. It is an update on the cooperation between the Federation and our "White Knights", who are working toward eliminating the power of the illuminati, and ultimately having NESARA announced, etc.

By accessing these books and sites, you will be able to greatly enlarge upon any of the things presented and revealed to you in this Book 1 of the "Are You A Mushroom" series.

What's Coming In Book 2 ?

1.) Area 51 has 27 levels. 16 manmade, and 11 deeper and older by earlier civilization.

2.) Content & Significance of the 3rd., prophesy given at Fatima.

3.) Inner Earth (2 sources) – 7 civilizations, people described – clean environment, etc.

4.) Nazi camps in Germany tied currently back to a plan to impose Marshal Law in the U.S., including 600+ prison camps already in place in the U.S.

5.) Water Powered Automobiles, & various Brown's Gas generators. Stan Meyer, who first publicised his water powered dune buggy, was assassinated by poisoning. Builders of gas generators threatened, as far away as in India, etc.

6.) Magnet Motors, one at 160% efficiency, and one at 700%

Those are some of the first main items now being laid out for **Book 2,** and many more interesting things will follow that need to be revealed. The author has access to so many things that it is a matter of priorities as to what gets into book 2, or later in this sequence..